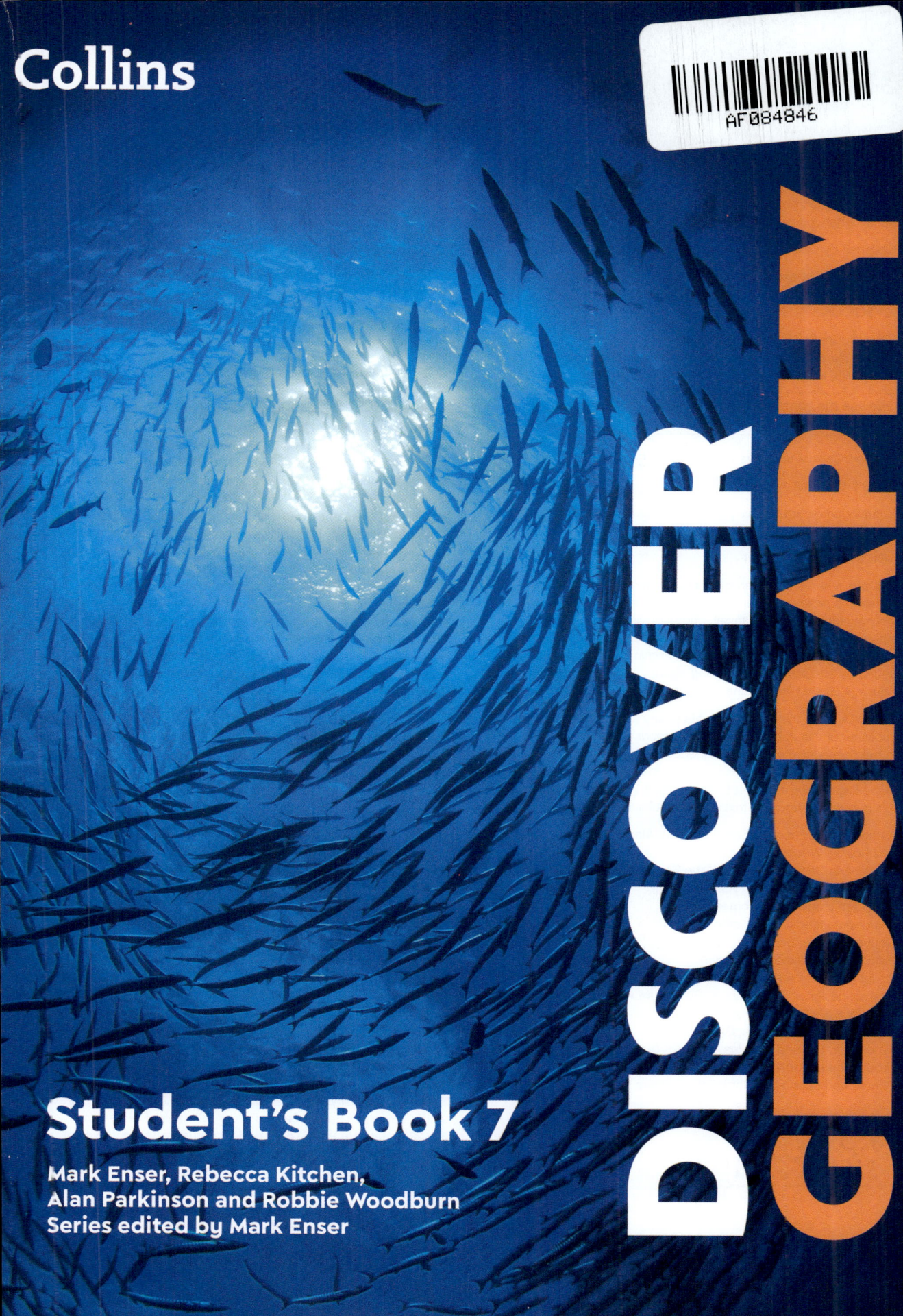

William Collins' dream of knowledge for all began with the publication of his first book in 1819.

A self-educated mill worker, he not only enriched millions of lives, but also founded a flourishing publishing house. Today, staying true to this spirit, Collins books are packed with inspiration, innovation and practical expertise.

They place you at the centre of a world of possibility and give you exactly what you need to explore it.

Published by Collins

An imprint of HarperCollins*Publishers*
The News Building, 1 London Bridge Street, London,
SE1 9GF, UK

HarperCollins*Publishers*
Macken House, 39/40 Mayor Street Upper, Dublin 1,
D01 C9W8, Ireland

Browse the complete Collins catalogue at
collins.co.uk

© HarperCollins*Publishers* Limited 2026

10 9 8 7 6 5 4 3 2 1

A catalogue record for this publication is available from the British Library.

ISBN 978-0-00-878320-4

All rights reserved. No part of this publication may be reproduced, stored in a retrieval system, or transmitted in any form by any means, electronic, mechanical, photocopying, recording or otherwise, without the prior written permission of the Publisher or a licence permitting restricted copying in the United Kingdom issued by the Copyright Licensing Agency Ltd, 5th Floor, Shackleton House, 4 Battle Bridge Lane, London SE1 2HX.

Without limiting the exclusive rights of any author, contributor or the publisher of this publication, any unauthorised use of this publication to train generative artificial intelligence (AI) technologies is expressly prohibited. HarperCollins also exercise their rights under Article 4(3) of the Digital Single Market Directive 2019/790 and expressly reserve this publication from the text and data mining exception.

Authors: Mark Enser, Rebecca Kitchen, Alan Parkinson and Robbie Woodburn
Publishers: Cathy Martin and Katie Sergeant
Product manager: Saaleh Patel
Project manager: Just Content
Development editor: Jo Kemp
Copyeditor: Jan Schubert
Proofreader: Rebecca Ramsden
Cover designer: Amparo Kneath, Kneath Associates
Internal designer: Steve Evans, Planet Life Art
Illustrator: Six Red Marbles
Cartography: Gordon MacGilp
Typesetter: Six Red Marbles
Production controller: Alhady Ali
Printed and bound by: Martins the Printers

## Acknowledgements

The publishers gratefully acknowledge the permission granted to reproduce the copyright material in this book. Every effort has been made to trace copyright holders and to obtain their permission for the use of copyright material. The publishers will gladly receive any information enabling them to rectify any error or omission at the first opportunity.

(t = top, c = center, b = bottom, r = right, l = left)

### Images

Front cover Rich Carey/Shutterstock, p6t Ashvin Mistry/Alamy, p28 malinikart/Alamy, p30b Nazmul Islam/Alamy, p34t Xinhua/Alamy, p34bl Jia Qi/Alamy, p34br xPACIFICA/Alamy, p36r Genevieve Vallee/Alamy, p111 Planetary Health Check. All other photos © Shutterstock.com

### Text

We are grateful to the following for permission to reproduce copyright material:

p.5 – Figure 1.6. Riyadh Climate Graph, data produced by Climate Data – Saudi Arabia 29. p.12 – Figure 1.7 Changes in global average temperature over the last 450,000 years. Taken from: Glacial-interglacial cycles over the past 450,000 years. Produced by Noaa – National Centers for Environmental Information. Attribution 4.0 International CC BY 4.0 Deed. p.12 – Figure 1.8 Changes in global average temperature and CO2 concentration since 1880. Produced by Noaa – National Centers for Environmental information. Attribution 4.0 International CC BY 4.0 Deed. p.13 – Figure 1.19 Temperature projections for the future based on emissions. Produced by GlobalChange.gov. Attribution 4.0 International CC BY 4.0 Deed. p.15 – Figure 1.21 Large volcanic eruptions – Volcanoes, weather and climate, courtesy of the Hong Kong Observatory of HKSAR. p.16 – Figure 1.22 Temperature and CO2 the last 800,000 years. Taken from Earth's Average Temperature and Green House Gas Concentrations with data provided by Ben Henley and Nerilie Abram. p.73 – Figure 4.19 Graph for climate in Oymyakon (Siberia) was produced by Climates To Travel – © climatestotravel.com. p.87 – Figure 5.4 Global Population Growth, 1950-2023, Data source: UN, World Population Prospects (2024) Attribution 4.0 International CC BY 4.0 Deed. p.87 – Figure 5.5 The total value of agricultural production for countries, 2023 Food and Agriculture Organization of the United Nations (2025) – with major processing by Our World in Data. Attribution 4.0 International CC BY 4.0 Deed. p.89 – Figure 5.7 The United Nations' definition of food security. (World Food Summit 1996) Reasonable Endeavours. p.89 – Table 5.1 Countries with the highest and lowest Global Food Security Index scores in 2022. September 2022. © Adapted from a chart, originally published by Economist Impact, London 2022. p.98 – Table 5.2 Number of emergency food parcels distributed by food banks in the Trussell Community. © Trussell. p.109 – Figure 6.8 Possible climate tipping points. Version 1.1, 2023. Attribution 4.0 International CC BY 4.0 Deed. p.111 – Figure 6.9 The health of the planet. From: The Health of the Planet 2025. © Potsdam Institute for Climate Impact Research (PIK) / GLOBAÏA. p.112 – Figure 6.10 Are extreme events becoming more frequent as a result of climate change? metoffice.gov.uk © Crown Copyright. p.119 – Figure 6.19 The inequity of climate change. Data compiled by Marshall Burke, Professor, Doerr School of Sustainability | Center on Food Security and the Environment – Stanford University and Noah Diffenbaugh, William Wrigley professor and Kimmelman Family Senior Fellow - Stanford. Sourced from his 2019 paper in PNAS. p.120 – 6.20 Climate change, the great displacer. Produced by Statista Charts, statistics portal for market data. Attribution 4.0 International CC BY 4.0 Deed. p.123 – Figure 6.25 Melting arctic ice is making shipping routes more accessible. "Adapted from Malte Humpert/The Arctic Institute." p.124 – Figure 6.27 The world cities that are most at risk from sea-level rise. Produced by Statista Charts, statistics portal for market data – source Climate Central. Attribution 4.0 International CC BY 4.0 Deed.

# Contents

## Introduction: How to use this book — v

## Chapter 1: Why does climate change? — 2

- 1.1 What is climate? — 4
- 1.2 Why is temperature different in different places? — 6
- 1.3 Why is rainfall different in different places? — 8
- 1.4 How do you know what the climate is like? — 10
- 1.5 How has climate changed over time? — 12
- 1.6 Does climate change naturally? — 14
- 1.7 How have humans changed the climate? — 16
- 1.8 Will climate change everywhere? — 18

## Chapter 2: How might climate change affect drainage basins? — 22

- 2.1 What are drainage basins and what is climate change? — 24
- 2.2 How does climate change affect water systems? — 26
- 2.3 What are the causes and effects of flooding? — 28
- 2.4 To what extent does climate change increase flood risk? — 30
- 2.5 What are the causes and effects of drought? — 32
- 2.6 In what ways can drought management strategies mitigate climate change? — 34
- 2.7 What is salination and how is it affected by climate change? — 36
- 2.8 How can you use mapping and GIS to study drainage basins? — 38

## Chapter 3: Why does the Lake District look different from the Himalayas? — 43

- 3.1 How do landscapes form and change over time? — 45
- 3.2 What are the main differences and similarities between the Lake District and the Himalayas? — 47
- 3.3 How do climate and geography influence the plants and animals in each region? — 49
- 3.4 How have humans adapted to live in these diverse landscapes? — 51
- 3.5 What impact do human activities have on these environments? — 53
- 3.6 How do these landscapes influence culture and daily life? — 55
- 3.7 What environmental challenges do these regions face, and how are they being addressed? — 57
- 3.8 How can we appreciate and preserve diverse landscapes around the world? — 59

## Contents

### Chapter 4: How does life adapt to its environment? — 63

| | | | | | |
|---|---|---|---|---|---|
| 4.1 | How does climate affect the world's biomes? | 65 | 4.5 | What are the characteristics of cold desert biomes? | 73 |
| 4.2 | What are the characteristics of hot desert biomes? | 67 | 4.6 | How do people adapt to life in cold deserts? | 75 |
| 4.3 | How do people adapt to life in hot deserts? | 69 | 4.7 | What are the opportunities for people in cold deserts? | 77 |
| 4.4 | What are the opportunities for people in hot deserts? | 71 | 4.8 | What does the future hold for people living in extreme environments? | 79 |

### Chapter 5: What can be done to ensure everyone has enough food? — 85

| | | | | | |
|---|---|---|---|---|---|
| 5.1 | Is global food production keeping up with population growth? | 87 | 5.6 | How can a country improve its food security? | 97 |
| 5.2 | What is food security and why does it vary? | 89 | 5.7 | Why does it matter what people choose to eat? | 99 |
| 5.3 | Why is soil so important? | 91 | 5.8 | What impact might climate change have on future food production? | 101 |
| 5.4 | How are the world's soils changing? | 93 | | | |
| 5.5 | How does the global food supply system work? | 95 | | | |

### Chapter 6: What impacts will a changing climate have? — 105

| | | | | | |
|---|---|---|---|---|---|
| 6.1 | How can we classify the impacts of climate change? | 107 | 6.5 | What are some economic impacts of climate change? | 116 |
| 6.2 | What is the health of the planet? | 109 | 6.6 | What are some of the social impacts of climate change? | 118 |
| 6.3 | What are some environmental impacts of climate change? | 112 | 6.7 | What are climate refugees? | 120 |
| 6.4 | More environmental impacts of climate change | 114 | 6.8 | How will climate change impact Russia? | 122 |

### Glossary of key terms — 127

# Introduction: How to use this book

The Collins Discover Geography 7 Student's Book introduces you to Geography – the study of Earth's landscapes, people and environments, and how they connect. Each chapter develops your curiosity about the world around you and builds the knowledge and skills needed to think and act like a geographer.

The series is organised around nine key geographical concepts that help you understand our planet and your place in it. These are:

- **space** – understanding how and why places are arranged as they are on Earth
- **place** – exploring what makes each location unique and how people experience it
- **Earth systems** – discovering the natural processes that shape our landscapes and climates
- **environment** – investigating the relationships between people and the natural world
- **time** – considering how places and environments change over different timescales
- **scale** – linking local, regional and global patterns and issues
- **diversity** – recognising the variety of cultures, landscapes and environments on Earth
- **interconnection** – examining how people, places and environments are linked
- **interpretation** – learning how evidence, data and viewpoints can be analysed and explained.

Each chapter builds knowledge and understanding through enquiry-based learning, practical activities and real-world case studies from across the globe. You will explore environments as varied as deserts, rainforests, cities and coastlines, and consider how people everywhere are shaping and responding to change. **End-of-chapter reviews** will test your understanding and apply what you have learned to new contexts, while **enquiry tasks** encourage you to think critically, solve problems and communicate your ideas clearly.

Discover Geography 7 takes an international approach and looks to the future – asking how we can live sustainably on a changing planet. It provides the foundation for your future geographical learning and helps you see the world through a geographer's eyes: connected, dynamic and full of possibility.

# Introduction: How to use this book

## Key features of the Student's Book

Each chapter opens with an explanation of why the topic is being studied and what you can expect to learn.

The chapter introduction highlights the parts of the world that you will be studying.

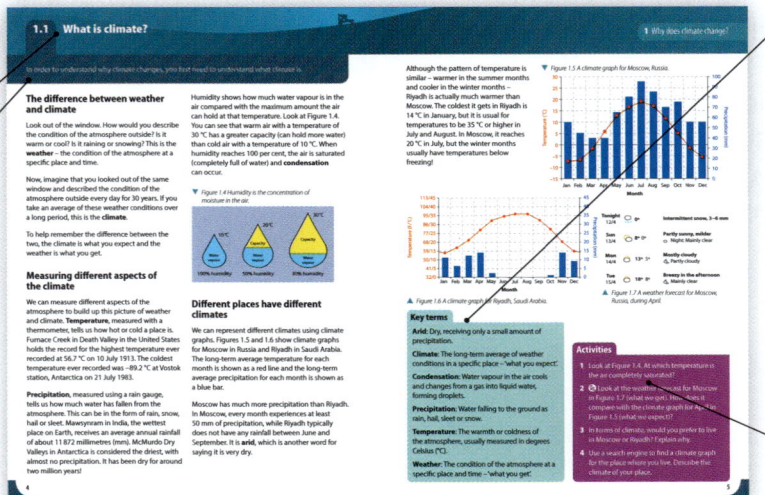

Each lesson is based on a question that should develop the knowledge to answer it.

The lesson page starts by explaining why this is an important question to answer.

Each lesson explores the key terms that you should know for the activities.

You will find a range of activities to complete. Some involve using geographical skills. Look for the GS icon.

vi

# Introduction: How to use this book

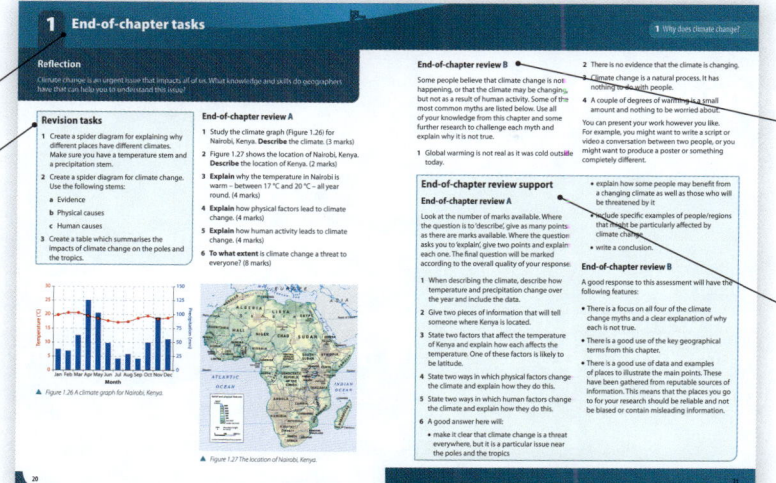

Every chapter ends with some summary tasks to complete.

You will find revision tasks that will help you prepare for these activities.

End-of-chapter reviews include options for short tests and longer independent pieces of work.

You will find support and advice in each review section.

# 1 Why does climate change?

## Chapter overview

### Why are you studying this?
Climate change is one of the most important issues of our time. It shapes the physical environment and impacts human societies.

### Skills
In this chapter, you will learn about:
- climate graphs and how to interpret them
- graphs that show patterns of data in past, present and future trends.

### Learning outcomes
By the end of this chapter, you will understand:
- the difference between weather and climate
- that different places have different climates and why this is the case
- that the climate has changed over time and the evidence for this
- the physical and human factors that have caused climate change
- which parts of the world will be most affected by climate change.

## What are the connections?
An understanding of climate change underpins many aspects of geography. You will be able to apply what you learn here in most of the following chapters.

In Chapter 6, you will look at the impacts of a changing climate, and in *Discover Geography 9*, Chapter 2, you will explore how we can respond to climate change.

## Where are you going?
As well as looking at climate change generally, you will be introduced to the climates of Russia and the Middle East and, specifically, Saudi Arabia. You will learn more about how climate change is impacting Russia in Chapter 6. In *Discover Geography 9*, Chapter 2, you will consider responses to climate change in the Middle East.

◀ Figure 1.1 Map of the world showing the locations of Russia and Saudi Arabia.

**1 Why does climate change?**

## Variable climates

Some places in the world have extreme climates where it is very hot or cold, or wet or dry. Other places have a temperate climate which does not have extremes.

Climate change will affect both extreme and temperate climates to some extent. However, it is likely to impact extreme hot climates the most.

◀ Figure 1.2 January is the coldest month in Moscow, Russia.

◀ Figure 1.3 In Riyadh, Saudi Arabia, temperatures can reach 45 °C in August.

### Discuss

1  How would you describe the climate where you live? How does it affect you?
2  What do you know about climate change already?
3  How do you feel about climate change?

# 1.1 What is climate?

In order to understand why climate changes, you first need to understand what climate is.

## The difference between weather and climate

Look out of the window. How would you describe the condition of the atmosphere outside? Is it warm or cool? Is it raining or snowing? This is the **weather** – the condition of the atmosphere at a specific place and time.

Now, imagine that you looked out of the same window and described the condition of the atmosphere outside every day for 30 years. If you take an average of these weather conditions over a long period, this is the **climate**.

To help remember the difference between the two, the climate is what you expect and the weather is what you get.

## Measuring different aspects of the climate

We can measure different aspects of the atmosphere to build up this picture of weather and climate. **Temperature**, measured with a thermometer, tells us how hot or cold a place is. Furnace Creek in Death Valley in the United States holds the record for the highest temperature ever recorded at 56.7 °C on 10 July 1913. The coldest temperature ever recorded was −89.2 °C at Vostok station, Antarctica on 21 July 1983.

**Precipitation**, measured using a rain gauge, tells us how much water has fallen from the atmosphere. This can be in the form of rain, snow, hail or sleet. Mawsynram in India, the wettest place on Earth, receives an average annual rainfall of about 11 872 millimetres (mm). McMurdo Dry Valleys in Antarctica is considered the driest, with almost no precipitation. It has been dry for around two million years!

Humidity shows how much water vapour is in the air compared with the maximum amount the air can hold at that temperature. Look at Figure 1.4. You can see that warm air with a temperature of 30 °C has a greater capacity (can hold more water) than cold air with a temperature of 10 °C. When humidity reaches 100 per cent, the air is saturated (completely full of water) and **condensation** can occur.

▼ Figure 1.4 Humidity is the concentration of moisture in the air.

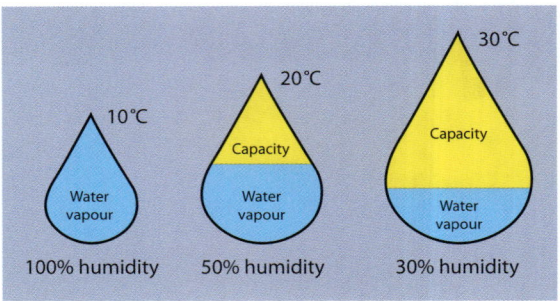

## Different places have different climates

We can represent different climates using climate graphs. Figures 1.5 and 1.6 show climate graphs for Moscow in Russia and Riyadh in Saudi Arabia. The long-term average temperature for each month is shown as a red line and the long-term average precipitation for each month is shown as a blue bar.

Moscow has much more precipitation than Riyadh. In Moscow, every month experiences at least 50 mm of precipitation, while Riyadh typically does not have any rainfall between June and September. It is **arid**, which is another word for saying it is very dry.

# 1 Why does climate change?

Although the pattern of temperature is similar – warmer in the summer months and cooler in the winter months – Riyadh is actually much warmer than Moscow. The coldest it gets in Riyadh is 14 °C in January, but it is usual for temperatures to be 35 °C or higher in July and August. In Moscow, it reaches 20 °C in July, but the winter months usually have temperatures below freezing!

Figure 1.5 A climate graph for Moscow, Russia.

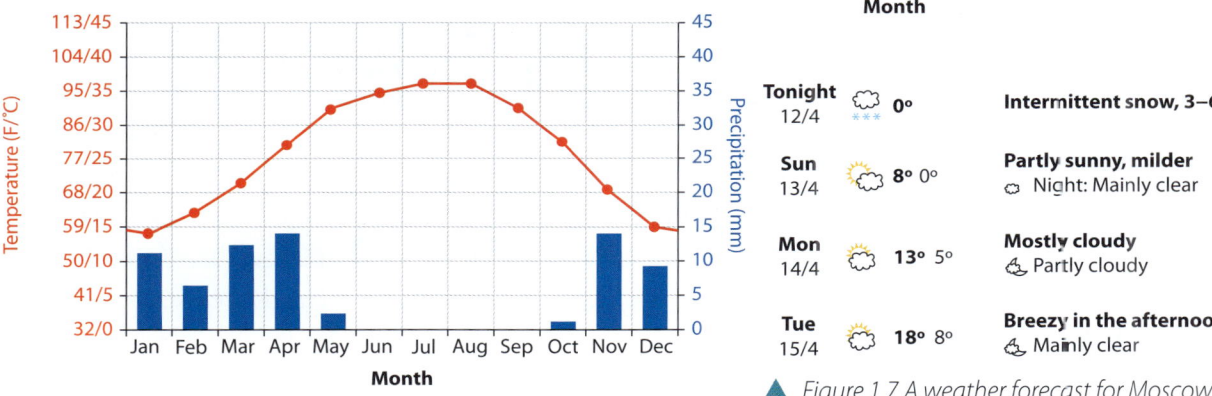

Figure 1.6 A climate graph for Riyadh, Saudi Arabia.

Figure 1.7 A weather forecast for Moscow, Russia, during April.

## Key terms

**Arid**: Dry, receiving only a small amount of precipitation.

**Climate**: The long-term average of weather conditions in a specific place – 'what you expect'.

**Condensation**: Water vapour in the air cools and changes from a gas into liquid water, forming droplets.

**Precipitation**: Water falling to the ground as rain, hail, sleet or snow.

**Temperature**: The warmth or coldness of the atmosphere, usually measured in degrees Celsius (°C).

**Weather**: The condition of the atmosphere at a specific place and time – 'what you get'.

## Activities

1 Look at Figure 1.4. At which temperature is the air completely saturated?

2 Look at the weather forecast for Moscow in Figure 1.7 (what we get). How does it compare with the climate graph for April in Figure 1.5 (what we expect)?

3 In terms of climate, would you prefer to live in Moscow or Riyadh? Explain why.

4 Use a search engine to find a climate graph for the place where you live. Describe the climate of your place.

# 1.2 Why is temperature different in different places?

In this lesson, you will look at reasons for differences in temperature in different places. You will apply this knowledge in future chapters, particularly Chapter 4, when you will look at how climate affects the world's biomes.

## Introducing different climate zones

Look at Figure 1.9 showing the world's climate zones. You can see that Moscow has a cold **temperate climate** – cool summers and cold winters – while Riyadh has a tropical desert climate – hot and extremely dry throughout the year. Notice the major lines of latitude that divide the world. They are imaginary lines, but if you visit some places on the equator (0° – it cuts the Earth in half), you can stand with one foot in the northern hemisphere and the other foot in the southern hemisphere!

▲ Figure 1.8 The equator in Ecuador marks 0° latitude. Ecuador literally means 'equator' in Spanish!

These lines help us understand the location of different climate zones. Places on the equator have an equatorial climate, while places on the tropics of Cancer and Capricorn have a dry, desert climate like Riyadh.

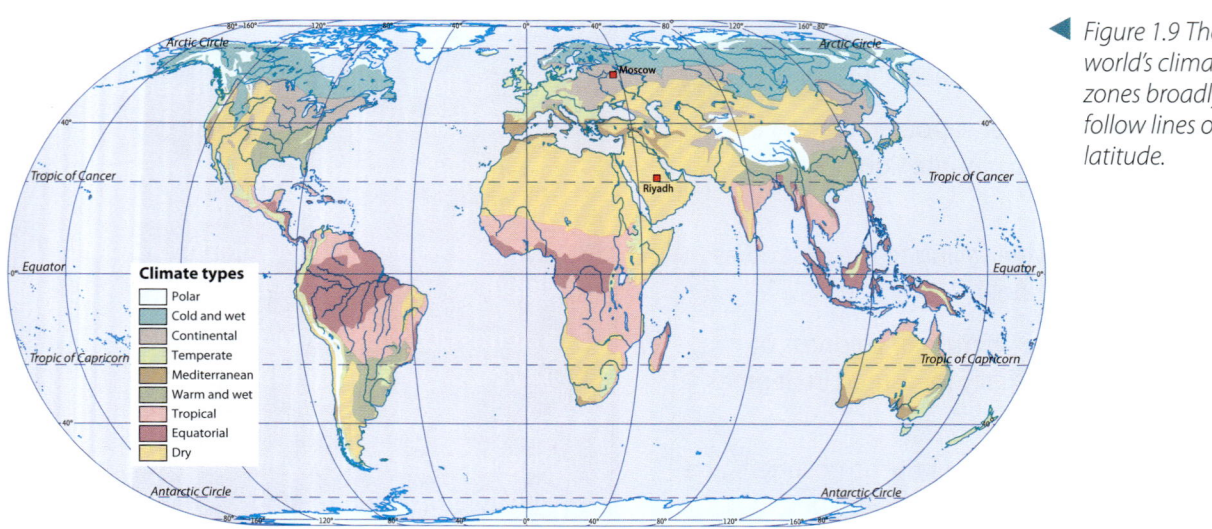

◄ Figure 1.9 The world's climate zones broadly follow lines of latitude.

# 1 Why does climate change?

## Factors affecting temperature

It is warmer at the equator than at the poles. Many people think this is because the equator is closer to the Sun. It is about 21.5 kilometres (km) closer, but when you understand that the Sun is 149 million km from the Earth, it makes absolutely no difference! Instead, you can see from Figure 1.10 that the Earth is tilted slightly. It is also a sphere and has a curved surface. Therefore, the Sun's rays are more spread out at the poles and are more concentrated at the equator – this is why it is warmer there.

However, there are also other more local factors that affect temperature. **Altitude** is a significant factor – for every 100 metres (m) you rise above sea level, it is about 1 °C cooler (see Figure 1.11). This is because as altitude increases, **air pressure** decreases, causing the air to expand and lose heat, which lowers the temperature. This is why Mount Kenya, which is located just 9° south of the equator, has snow on it all year round.

Distance from the sea can also affect temperature. Land is solid and has opaque (not see-through) surfaces. The Sun's rays heat it up quickly during the day. However, at night, when there is no sunlight, the land loses its heat quickly too. The opposite happens to the seas and oceans. It takes a long time for water to heat up because oceans are deep and the water is always moving. It also takes a long time for oceans to lose their heat. This means that places near the coast have more moderate temperatures. Places further inland have more extreme temperatures.

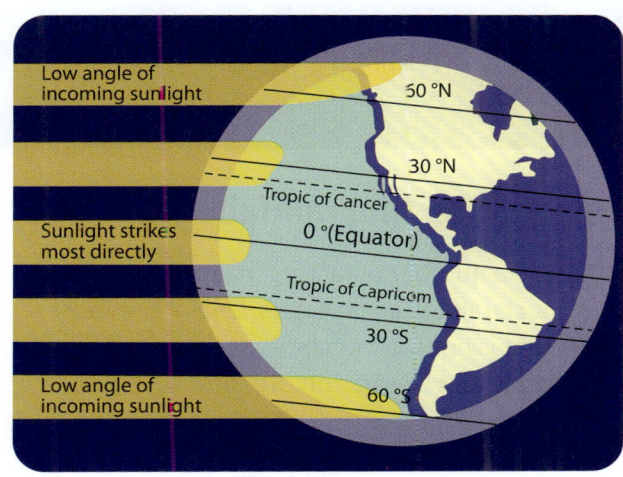

▲ Figure 1.10 The Sun's rays hit the Earth at an angle. This means they are more concentrated at the equator than at the poles.

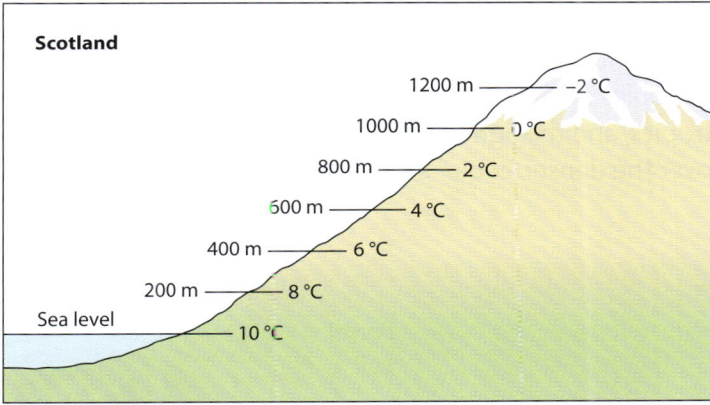

▲ Figure 1.11 Altitude has a significant impact on temperature. The higher you go, the colder it gets.

### Key terms

**Air pressure**: Force from the weight of the air above a place on the Earth's surface.

**Altitude**: Height above sea level. Mountains have a high altitude.

**Temperate climate**: A climate with moderate temperatures, not too hot or too cold.

### Activities

1. Look at Figure 1.9. Which climate zone do you live in?

2. What is the latitude of the place where you live? You can look at an atlas to help you be accurate.

3. Look at Figure 1.10. If the answer is, 'Because of the tilt and curvature of the Earth which means that the Sun's rays are more concentrated at the equator and more spread out at the poles', what is the question?

7

## 1.3 Why is rainfall different in different places?

In this lesson, you will look at reasons for differences in rainfall. You will apply this knowledge in future chapters, particularly Chapter 4, when you will look at how climate affects the world's biomes.

### Factors affecting rainfall

There are a number of factors that influence how much rainfall a place gets. One of the most important is how air circulates around the Earth and the **impact** this has on pressure.

You will see in Figure 1.12 that, at the equator, the air is warm and rises. This air moves north and south into higher latitudes and, as it does so, it gets cooler. The air starts to sink at around 30° north and south. The air continues to travel into higher latitudes and starts to rise again at 60° north and south. This happens because air from the poles meets air which has travelled from the tropics, and the lighter, warm air is forced to rise over the denser, cooler air.

This pattern of rising and falling air creates different cells (Hadley cells near the equator, polar cells at the North and South Poles, and Ferrel cells in between). In places where there is low pressure, the air rises, cools and condenses to form rainclouds, so these areas get lots of rain. This explains why there are rainforests close to the equator. In places where there is high pressure, the air sinks, gets warmer and can hold more moisture, so these places are dry. This explains why there are deserts at around 30° north and south of the equator.

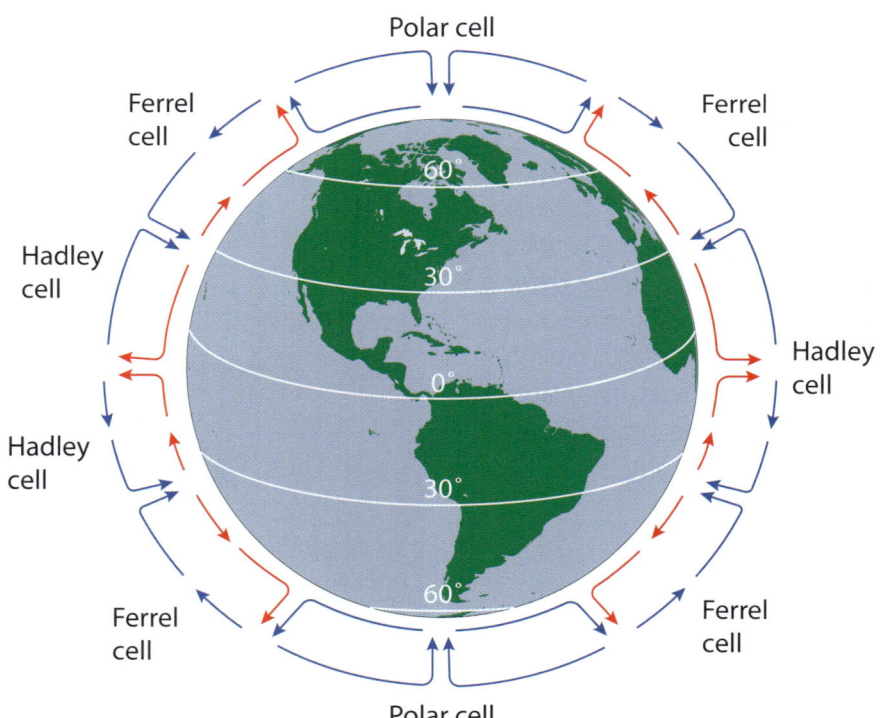

▲ *Figure 1.12 The global atmospheric circulation model describes how air of different temperatures is moved around the Earth.*

# 1 Why does climate change?

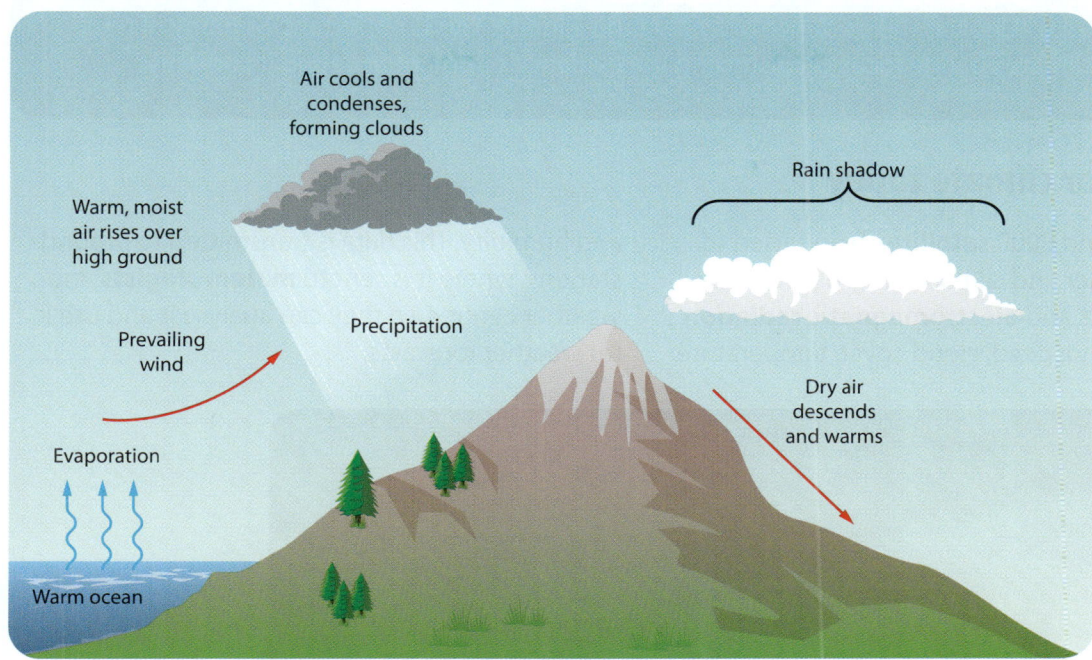

▲ Figure 1.13 Relief rainfall occurs in places which have hills or mountains.

Altitude also plays an important part in levels of rainfall. When air meets a mountain, it is forced to rise over it (see Figure 1.13). As air rises, it cools and condenses to form rainclouds, so there tends to be rain on the **windward** side of the mountain. On the other side, the air is dry and starts to descend and warm. This explains why one side of a mountain range tends to have more rainfall than the other. For example, the Pennines is a mountain range which runs down the centre of the UK. The west of the country is on the windward side of the Pennines and gets around 2000 mm of rainfall per year, while the east of the country gets around 600 mm. We call this type of rainfall, **relief** rainfall.

Areas near large bodies of water also tend to get more rainfall, as there is more water available to be evaporated, so the air holds more water. The direction of the **prevailing wind** can also be a factor. If it blows over water, it will bring moist air and rainfall. However, if it blows over land, the air will be dry and there will be less chance of rain.

### Key terms

**Impact**: The effect or influence something has on a person or place.

**Prevailing wind**: A wind that blows mostly from the same direction.

**Relief**: The shape of the land. For example, hills and mountains.

**Windward**: The side of a mountain that faces the prevailing wind.

### Activities

1. Look at Figure 1.12. Why are deserts at 30° north and south of the equator? Can you use an atlas to name some?

2. Find the Pennine range in an atlas. Can you explain why the east of the UK is drier than the west?

3. In Lesson 1.1, you used a search engine to find a climate graph for the place where you live. Can you now use all of the information in this lesson, and the previous one, to explain why your place has this climate?

## 1.4 How do you know what the climate is like?

In this lesson you will look at the evidence of a changing climate. This is important, as many of the myths around climate change focus on distorting the evidence or not interpreting it correctly.

### Evidence for climate today

There are around 8000 **satellites** being used to monitor weather and climate. They use remote sensing sensors and **electromagnetic radiation** to measure windspeed, cloud cover, temperature and humidity. This data is transmitted to ground stations, where it is sent to **meteorologists** and weather centres, so they can analyse it and use it for weather forecasts.

▲ Figure 1.14 Satellites send weather data to meteorologists.

The first weather satellite was launched by NASA in 1960, so how do you know what the climate was like before then? Most countries have a network of ground stations. These have been around since the 17th century, when instruments like the barometer and thermometer were invented and meant that accurate weather data could be collected.

### Evidence for past climate data

For evidence of what the climate was like hundreds or even thousands of years ago, you can look at ice cores, trees rings and ocean sediments. Ice cores are drilled from **glaciers** and ice sheets and contain layers that trap ancient air bubbles. By analysing the gases (like $CO_2$) in these bubbles, scientists can work out past temperatures going back hundreds of thousands of years. Figure 1.15 shows an ice core taken from a glacier in Iceland. This core has a series of dark layers. Each of these is ash from volcanic eruptions, giving us a record that goes back centuries.

# 1 Why does climate change?

▲ Figure 1.15 An ice core taken from a glacier in Iceland.

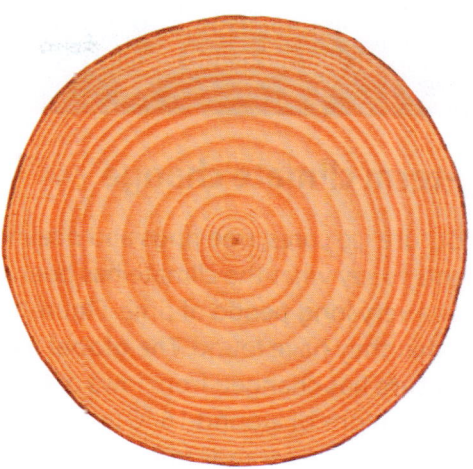

▲ Figure 1.16 Tree rings can tell us about past climates.

Tree rings can also tell us what the climate was like in the past. Every year a tree grows, another ring is added. This means that if a tree is chopped down, you can see the rings inside the trunk and work out how old it was, as in Figure 1.16. If a year has lots of precipitation, the tree will grow quickly and the ring for that year will be thick. If a year is dry, the tree will not grow much and the ring for that year will be thin.

Ocean sediments provide evidence over millions of years! Small creatures, mud, dust and organic material slowly settle on the sea floor as layers of **sediment**. Scientists take cores of these sediments and, because different organisms have adapted to survive in different climates, the layers tell us about the environment when they were laid down.

## Predicting the future

Evidence about climate in the past and in the present can help you know what the future has in store. Scientists feed this data into advanced computer programs called climate models. They are continually being improved with better data and artificial intelligence, so the predictions are becoming even more detailed and reliable.

### Key terms

**Electromagnetic radiation:** Energy that travels through space.

**Glacier:** A large, slow-moving mass of ice.

**Meteorologist:** A scientist who studies the Earth's atmosphere to understand, observe and predict the weather and climate.

**Satellite:** An object that orbits around a larger body in space.

**Sediment:** Solid material made of grains or fragments of rock that build up in layers.

### Activities

1 Look at Figure 1.15. How many volcanic eruptions took place in Iceland that are evidenced in the ice core?

2 Look at Figure 1.16. Can you suggest **two** conclusions that you can draw from this data?

3 A meteorologist is a weather and climate scientist. What skills do you think a meteorologist might have?

## 1.5 How has climate changed over time?

To put what is happening at the moment into context, you need to understand that there have been periods of warming and cooling in the past.

### Long-term climate change

Scientists use ice cores, tree rings and ocean sediments to say what the climate has been like over a very long period of time. Figure 1.17 shows what they have found. The **global average temperature** has changed from lows of 8 °C (glacials), to highs of around 16 °C (interglacials). During a glacial, ice extends from the poles to cover more of the Earth's surface, while during an interglacial, it retreats to cover only the poles. For example, during the glacial that happened 450 000 years ago, ice covered London. There is a fairly regular pattern of glacials and interglacials that repeats every 100 000 years or so.

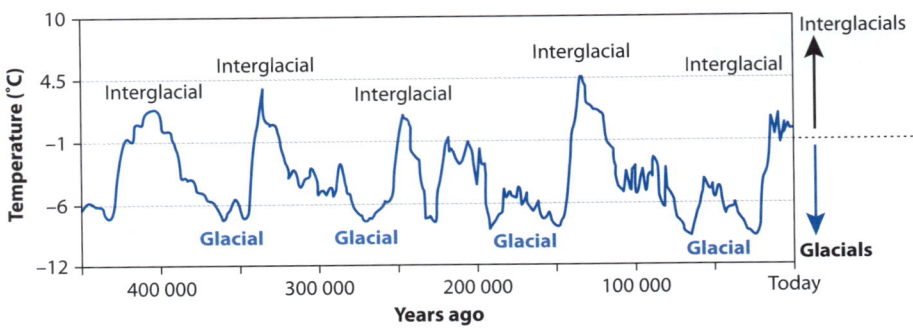

Figure 1.17 Changes in global average temperature over the last 450 000 years. You can see peaks (interglacials), and periods of lower global average temperature (glacials).

### Climate change since 1850

Looking at these long-term changes in the climate, you could assume that we are currently living in an interglacial, and that in the next 10 000 to 20 000 years the global average temperature is likely to cool back to glacial conditions. However, if you zoom in to a similar graph (Figure 1.18), which shows only the last 150 years, you can see that this is not what is happening.

The **pre-industrial average** (the average global temperature between 1850 and 1900) was 13.7 °C. However, since then, temperatures have started to climb at a rapid **rate**. The global average temperature in 2024 was the warmest on record, reaching about 1.55 °C above this pre-industrial level, and on 22 July 2024, the daily global average temperature hit a record high of 17.16 °C.

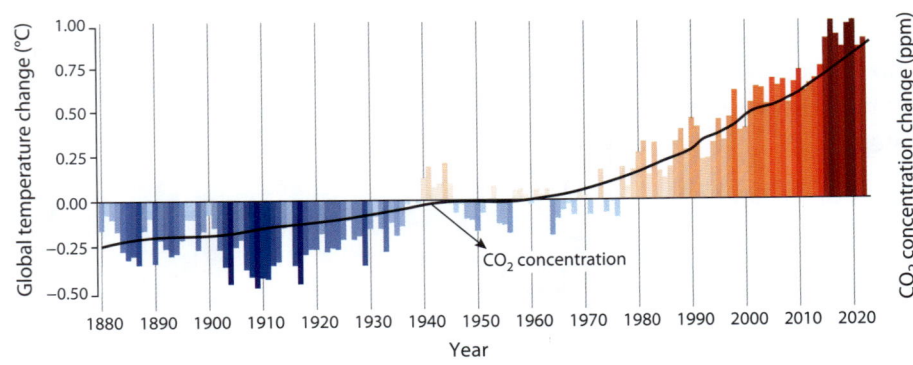

Figure 1.18 Changes in global average temperature and $CO_2$ concentration since 1880.

There seems to be a very strong relationship between the amount of $CO_2$ (carbon dioxide) in the atmosphere and the increase in temperature.

## Predicting the future

What does climate modelling look like? Figure 1.19 shows three possible futures: one with lower **emissions**, one with higher emissions and another with even higher emissions. The scenario with lower emissions would limit the global average temperature increase to well below 2 °C above the pre-industrial baseline of 13.7 °C. The higher emissions scenario suggests that, by 2100, global average temperatures will be 4 °C higher, while the even higher emissions scenario projects that it will be between 4.4 °C and 5 °C by 2100.

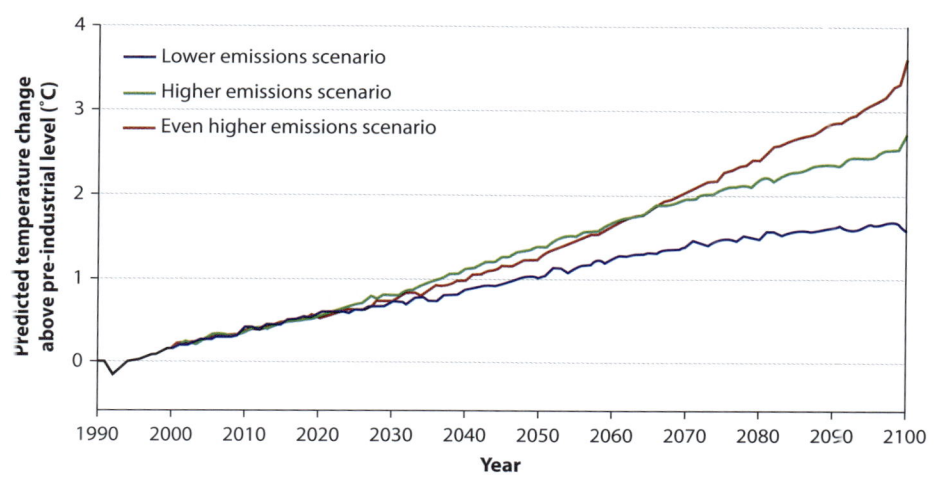

Figure 1.19 Predication of what might happen to the temperature in the future, depending on the level of emissions.

### Key terms

**Emissions**: Substances, usually gases, released into the atmosphere from human activities.

**Global average temperature**: The average of Earth's surface temperatures, combining measurements from land and oceans.

**Pre-industrial average**: The average global temperature between 1850 and 1900, used as the baseline for measuring climate change.

**Rate**: In this case, the speed of change.

### Activities

1. Look at Figure 1.17. How many glacials and interglacials has the Earth experienced over the last 450 000 years?

2. Sketch what you might expect Figure 1.17 to look like for the next 100 000 years if these cycles keep repeating.

3. Look at Figure 1.18. Describe what is happening to both global average temperature and to $CO_2$ concentration.

4. Figure 1.19 shows three possible scenarios for the future. Which do you think would be the preferable scenario? Why do you think this?

5. What evidence is there to suggest that these projections might be correct?

## 1.6 Does climate change naturally?

In this lesson, you will start to consider the natural processes which caused the pattern of glacials and interglacials we saw in the previous lesson.

### Milankovitch cycles

Milutin Milankovitch was a Serbian scientist born in 1879. He looked at the evidence for long-term climate change (which we saw in Figure 1.17) and developed a theory to explain the pattern. He suggested that there are long-term, natural variations in the Earth's orbit around the Sun and the tilt on its **axis**, which affect how much energy it receives from the Sun. As we know from Lesson 1.2, this is one of the main influences affecting temperature.

The three main **Milankovitch cycles** shown in Figure 1.20 are:

- Eccentricity (100 000-year cycle): Changes in the shape of Earth's orbit around the Sun, from more circular to more elliptical (egg-shaped). This changes the distance between the Earth and the Sun and the amount of energy the Earth receives from the Sun.

- Obliquity (41 000-year cycle): Changes in the tilt of Earth's axis, which affects the intensity of the seasons. A greater tilt means more extreme seasons.

- Precession (about 23 000–26 000-year cycle): The wobble in Earth's axis, which changes the timing of the seasons.

These cycles influence the sunlight that reaches the Earth's surface, especially in high latitudes in the northern hemisphere. They affect the pattern of glacials and interglacials, but only very slowly. They cannot explain the rapid change in temperature shown in Figure 1.18.

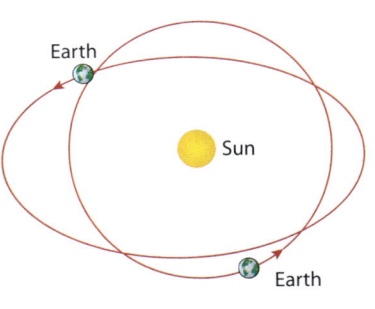
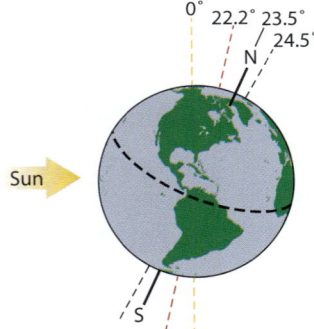
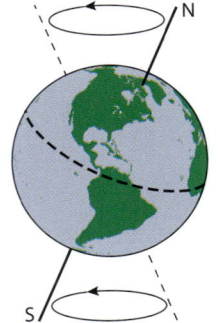

Figure 1.20 The three Milankovitch cycles of eccentricity, obliquity (tilt) and precession.

**Eccentricity** Earth encounters more variation in the energy that it receives from the Sun when Earth's orbit is elongated than it does when Earth's orbit is more circular.

**Obliquity (tilt)** The tilt of Earth's axis varies between 22.2° and 24.5°. The greater the tilt angle is, the more solar energy the poles receive.

**Precession** A gradual change, or 'wobble,' in the orientation of Earth's axis affects the relationship between Earth's tilt and eccentricity.

### Volcanic eruptions

Volcanic eruptions can also cause changes in climate. When a large and explosive volcano erupts, it releases huge amounts of sulphur gases into the atmosphere. These reflect sunlight back into space, which leads to a temporary cooling of the Earth (Figure 1.21). How long this cooling

# 1 Why does climate change?

lasts depends on the size of the eruption and the amount of sulphur dioxide ($SO_2$) released. For example, the 1991 eruption of Mount Pinatubo in the Philippines caused global temperatures to drop by as much as 0.5 °C for a couple of years. The cooling can lead to more snow and ice staying on the ground. These reflect even more sunlight, which can reinforce or extend the cooling effect. This is known as a **feedback loop**.

Volcanoes also release carbon dioxide, which is a **greenhouse gas** that can trap heat in the atmosphere. However, the amount of $CO_2$ from volcanoes is very small compared with what humans release by burning fossil fuels – oil, coal and gas made from the fossilised remains of plants and animals. So, volcanoes do not cause significant long-term warming compared with human activities.

## Sunspot activity

Sunspot activity is the increase and decrease in the number of dark spots on the Sun's surface, caused by intense magnetic activity. These cycles in sunspot activity last about 11 years and are linked to small changes in the amount of energy from the Sun. During periods of low sunspot activity, the Sun emits slightly less ultraviolet radiation than normal. The Maunder Minimum happened between 1645 and 1715 when sunspots were extremely rare, lowering global average temperatures by 0.4 °C.

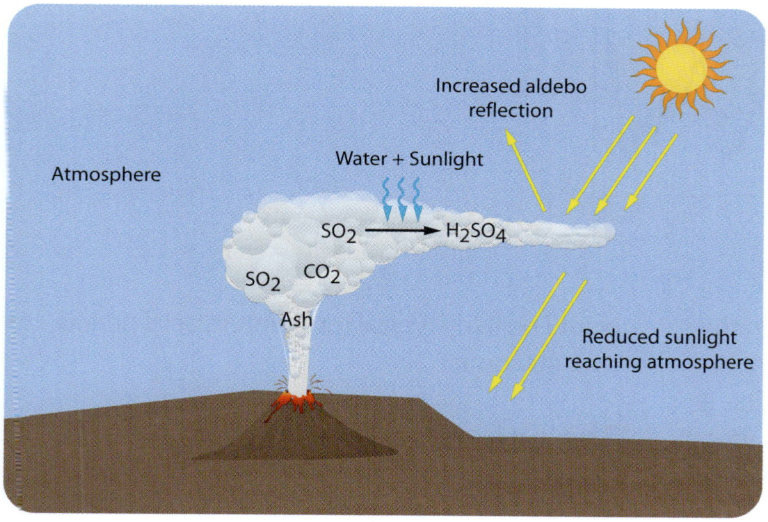

◀ Figure 1.21 Large volcanic eruptions can lead to global cooling – a volcanic winter.

## Key terms

**Axis**: An imaginary straight line that an object spins around. The Earth's axis runs through the North and South Poles.

**Feedback loop**: A process where a change triggers additional effects that reinforce or counteract the original change.

**Greenhouse gas**: A gas in the Earth's atmosphere that absorbs and traps heat.

**Milankovitch cycles**: Long-term, natural variations in Earth's orbit that affect how much solar energy the planet receives.

## Activities

1 Look at Figure 1.20. Explain how Milankovitch cycles help us to understand long-term changes in climate.

2 Carry out some research about Milutin Milankovitch. Why do you think some people did not believe his theory?

3 Search for 'solar activity space weather' in a search engine. Explore the sunspots that are visible on the Sun today. Do you think we are currently in a period of intense or weak sunspot activity?

# 1.7 How have humans changed the climate?

In this lesson, you explore the influence that humans have had on climate change since 1850.

## The increase in carbon dioxide ($CO_2$) in the atmosphere

Look back at Figure 1.18, which shows the relationship between $CO_2$ concentration in the atmosphere and temperature since 1880. Now have a look at Figure 1.22, which shows the same relationship over the last 800 000 years. What do you notice?

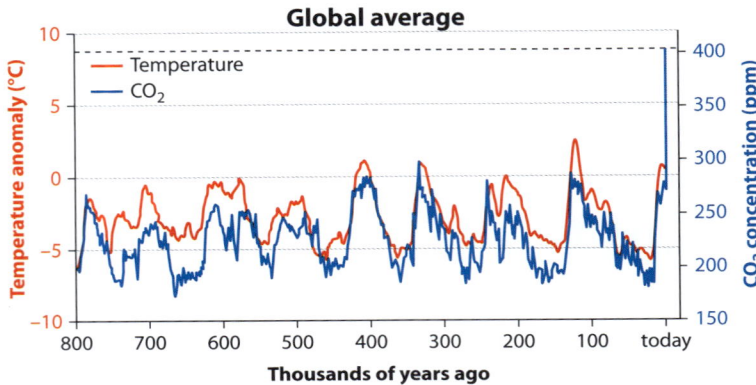

◀ Figure 1.22 Changes in global average temperature and $CO_2$ concentration over the last 800 000 years.

There is a very strong relationship between the concentration of $CO_2$ in the atmosphere and the global average temperature of the Earth. This is true over the shorter term (a few hundred years) and the longer term (a few hundred thousand years). However, you can also see that, since around 1850, there has been a sudden spike in the concentration of $CO_2$ in the atmosphere, from around 300 **parts per million (ppm)** – which would be fairly typical for an interglacial period – to over 400 ppm.

## The enhanced greenhouse effect

$CO_2$ is what we call a greenhouse gas. It is not the only one. Methane ($CH_4$), nitrous oxide ($N_2O$) and ozone ($O_3$) are greenhouse gases too. So is water vapour! These gases are produced naturally and act as the Earth's 'blanket'. They trap energy from the Sun and stop it escaping back into space (see Figure 1.23). We need these gases. Without them, Earth's average surface temperature would be around −18 °C, much too cold for plants, people and animals to survive.

Although this greenhouse effect is natural and necessary, human activities have increased the concentrations of greenhouse

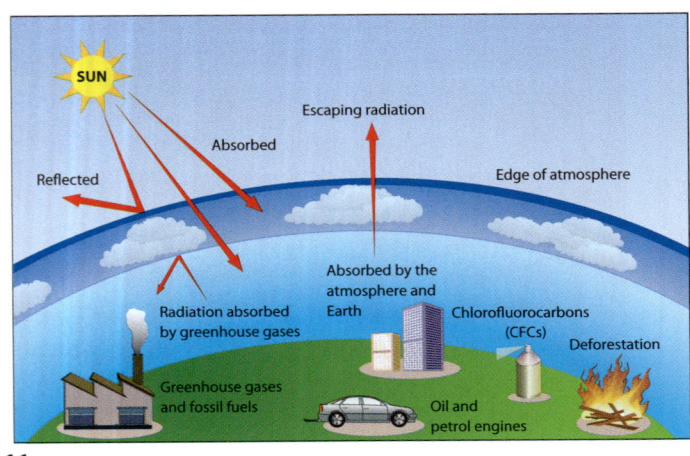

◀ Figure 1.23 The enhanced greenhouse effect.

# 1 Why does climate change?

gases in the atmosphere, including methane and nitrous oxide. We tend to focus on $CO_2$ because it the most abundant greenhouse gas emitted by humans and stays in the atmosphere for decades. (Other gases like methane break down more quickly and only stay in the atmosphere for between 8 and 12 years.)

This increase in greenhouse gases means that the 'blanket' around the Earth is getting thicker and trapping more heat. This **enhanced greenhouse effect** is why global average temperatures are increasing so quickly.

## Human activities and greenhouse gases

Although greenhouse gases exist in the atmosphere naturally, human activity since around 1850 has been responsible for their increase. Burning fossil fuels has been the biggest contributor. Although people have burnt coal as a source of energy for the last 5000 years, it has only been used on a large scale to generate electricity since 1760 and the start of the **Industrial Revolution**. We now use fossil fuels for electricity, heat, transportation and industry. Global fossil fuel consumption hit a record high in 2024, with a 1.5 per cent increase on 2023.

Deforestation, the cutting down of trees and forests, also has an impact as it reduces the Earth's capacity to absorb $CO_2$. At the same time, cutting down and burning trees releases stored carbon into the atmosphere. Farming activities, especially livestock, release methane (from manure) and nitrous oxide (from fertilised **soils**). This is one reason why environmental campaigners suggest that we have less meat in our diets.

### Key terms

**Enhanced greenhouse effect**: Increased warming of the Earth's atmosphere caused by higher concentrations of greenhouse gases due to human activities.

**Industrial Revolution**: A period of major economic and technological change that happened between 1750 and 1900, beginning in the UK.

**Parts per million (ppm)**: A unit of measurement that describes concentrations of $CO_2$ in the atmosphere.

**Soil**: The upper layer of earth in which plants grow.

### Activities

1. Use a search engine to search for 'Climesumer birth carbon calculator'. Input the year you were born into the tool. What was the concentration of $CO_2$ in the atmosphere then? What is it now? How much has the concentration grown since you were born?

2. Use Figure 1.23 to explain the enhanced greenhouse effect in your own words. Why do we use the term 'enhanced greenhouse effect' rather than just 'greenhouse effect'?

3. Carry out some research into the Industrial Revolution. Why do you think concentrations of $CO_2$ in the atmosphere started to increase soon afterwards?

## 1.8 Will climate change everywhere?

You now have all of the pieces in your enquiry jigsaw to explain how and why climate changes. You now need to zoom in and see if and how it will change in different parts of the world.

### Will climate change everywhere?

The short answer to this question is 'yes'. As a result of human activity, the climate everywhere on Earth will change. However, if you dig a little bit deeper, you realise the answer is a bit more complicated. Climate change is affecting every region on Earth, but not in the same way or at the same pace. Figure 1.24 shows which parts of the world are likely to have the greatest changes in temperature.

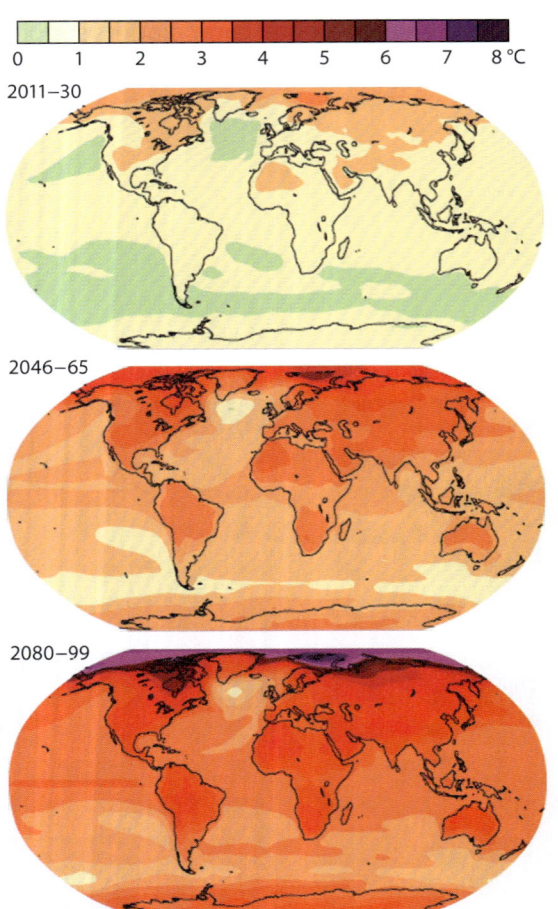

▲ Figure 1.24 Which parts of the Earth will see the greatest changes in temperature?

Nearly all regions are experiencing rising average temperatures, but the rate and amount differ. For example, the Arctic is warming about four times faster than the global average (3 °C since the 1980s) and some parts of it, such as the Eurasian Arctic Ocean, are warming at seven times the global average! This process is known as polar or Arctic amplification, because it amplifies or increases the effect of global warming.

A changing climate also brings more extreme weather. Although more frequent and intense heatwaves and drought might be expected, climate change also brings heavy rainfall and storms. However, the severity of these events will depend on the local climate and geography.

### Climate change at the poles

This rapid temperature increase is seen in both the Arctic and Antarctic and is mainly driven by positive feedback loops (which you learned about in Lesson 1.5). Ice and snow at the poles reflect energy from the Sun and are called high **albedo** surfaces. However, with rising temperatures, the ice and snow melt and are replaced by darker ocean or land surfaces that absorb energy from the Sun. This causes local temperatures to increase much more than they would have done. The more the temperatures increase, the more the ice and snow melt and sea levels rise. Since 1900, there has been a 60 per cent decline in sea ice at the poles, with 2025 recording the lowest winter maximum since satellite records began.

**Permafrost** or permanently frozen ground covers about 15 per cent of the Earth's land surface in places such as Alaska, Canada, Russia and the Qinghai-Tibet Plateau in China. As temperatures increase, this permafrost is also starting to melt,

# 1 Why does climate change?

◀ Figure 1.25 Melting permafrost can mean that buildings are at risk of sinking into the ground, known as subsidence.

releasing the stored greenhouse gases carbon dioxide and methane. This amplifies global warming even further and also causes subsidence (see Figure 1.25).

## Climate change in the tropics

While temperatures are not rising as quickly in the tropics as they are at the poles, the combination of increased heat and humidity will make it harder for people, animals and **ecosystems** to survive. For example, some models suggest that, in northern Australia, days above 35 °C could increase dramatically by 2090 under high-emission scenarios. This may lead to heatwaves, drought and wildfires in the tropics, which increase health risks, particularly for people who are **vulnerable**.

At the same time, **monsoon** rainfall in South Asia is expected to become more intense, which may increase the risk of flooding and also mean that it is harder to grow crops. However, changes in ocean circulation and the Hadley cell, which you explored in Lesson 1.2, could alter patterns of rainfall, making some areas wetter, but others drier.

### Key terms

**Albedo**: A measure of how much of the Sun's energy a surface reflects.

**Ecosystem**: A community of living organisms interacting with each other and their physical environment.

**Monsoon**: A season with heavy rainfall, common in some parts of the world.

**Permafrost**: Permanently frozen soil.

**Vulnerable**: A person or place that is more likely to be badly affected by the impacts of climate change.

### Activities

1. Look at Figure 1.24. How is the temperature projected to change in your country?
2. Draw a diagram to show why polar amplification is causing the Arctic and Antarctic to warm more quickly than other places.
3. Look at Figure 1.25. Can you suggest where in the world you think this photograph was taken? Why do you think this?
4. How might climate change affect the tropics?

# 1 End-of-chapter tasks

## Reflection

Climate change is an urgent issue that impacts all of us. What knowledge and skills do geographers have that can help you to understand this issue?

## Revision tasks

1 Create a spider diagram for explaining why different places have different climates. Make sure you have a temperature stem and a precipitation stem.

2 Create a spider diagram for climate change. Use the following stems:
   a Evidence
   b Physical causes
   c Human causes

3 Create a table which summarises the impacts of climate change on the poles and the tropics.

## End-of-chapter review A

1 Study the climate graph (Figure 1.26) for Nairobi, Kenya. **Describe** the climate. (3 marks)

2 Figure 1.27 shows the location of Nairobi, Kenya. **Describe** the location of Kenya. (2 marks)

3 **Explain** why the temperature in Nairobi is warm – between 17 °C and 20 °C – all year round. (4 marks)

4 **Explain** how physical factors lead to climate change. (4 marks)

5 **Explain** how human activity leads to climate change. (4 marks)

6 **To what extent** is climate change a threat to everyone? (8 marks)

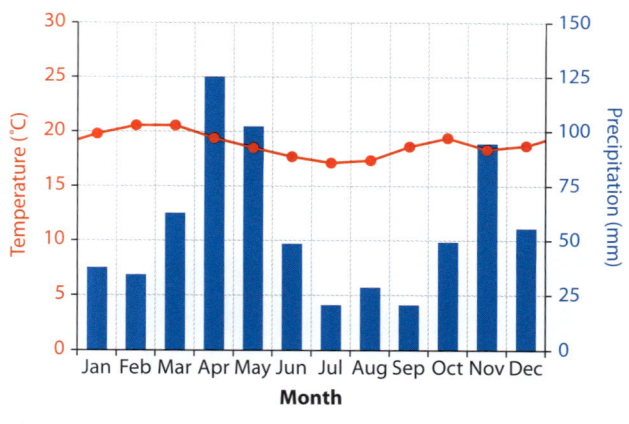

▲ Figure 1.26 A climate graph for Nairobi, Kenya.

▲ Figure 1.27 The location of Nairobi, Kenya.

## End-of-chapter review B

Some people believe that climate change is not happening, or that the climate may be changing, but not as a result of human activity. Some of the most common myths are listed below. Use all of your knowledge from this chapter and some further research to challenge each myth and explain why it is not true.

1 Global warming is not real as it was cold outside today.
2 There is no evidence that the climate is changing.
3 Climate change is a natural process. It has nothing to do with people.
4 A couple of degrees of warming is a small amount and nothing to be worried about.

You can present your work however you like. For example, you might want to write a script or video a conversation between two people, or you might want to produce a poster or something completely different.

## End-of-chapter review support

### End-of-chapter review A

Look at the number of marks available. Where the question is to 'describe', give as many points as there are marks available. Where the question asks you to 'explain', give two points and explain each one. The final question will be marked according to the overall quality of your response.

1 When describing the climate, describe how temperature and precipitation change over the year and include the data.
2 Give two pieces of information that will tell someone where Kenya is located.
3 State two factors that affect the temperature of Kenya and explain how each affects the temperature. One of these factors is likely to be latitude.
4 State two ways in which physical factors change the climate and explain how they do this.
5 State two ways in which human factors change the climate and explain how they do this.
6 A good answer here will:
   - make it clear that climate change is a threat everywhere, but it is a particular issue near the poles and the tropics
   - explain how some people may benefit from a changing climate as well as those who will be threatened by it
   - include specific examples of people/regions that might be particularly affected by climate change
   - write a conclusion.

### End-of-chapter review B

A good response to this assessment will have the following features:

- There is a focus on all four of the climate change myths and a clear explanation of why each is not true.
- There is a good use of the key geographical terms from this chapter.
- There is a good use of data and examples of places to illustrate the main points. These have been gathered from reputable sources of information. This means that the places you go to for your research should be reliable and not be biased or contain misleading information.

# 2 How might climate change affect drainage basins?

## Chapter overview

### Why are you studying this?

Changes in global weather patterns, as a result of climate change, can drastically affect the functioning of a drainage basin. You will explore how altered rainfall patterns and rising temperatures can cause significant environmental changes, and how these changes can affect the availability of water, ecosystems and human activities within and around drainage basins.

### Skills

In this chapter, you will learn about:
- how to read, understand and interpret information presented in maps, tables and graphs
- how to examine causality and consequence using real-world examples, to understand broader geographical concepts
- how location affects the availability of water, and that water resources are not distributed evenly
- how human activities can impact resources, including waste and conservation
- how to think critically about ways to save water.

### Learning outcomes

By the end of this chapter, you will understand:
- how human activities are affecting Earth's water cycle
- what that means for people and nature
- how to evaluate the specific impacts of climate, such as the frequency and severity of flooding and drought events
- effective mitigation and adaptation strategies to manage the impacts of climate change on drainage basins
- how changes in water availability due to climate change affect local ecosystems.

## What are the connections?

In Chapter 1, you learned how increased carbon dioxide levels in the atmosphere help explain why there might be more intense rainfall, leading to flooding in some drainage basins (Figure 2.1). This will help you understand how drainage basins are experiencing altered water cycles. In Chapter 4, you will explore how water availability affects the world's biomes. Then, in Chapter 6, you will learn more about the effects of climate change.

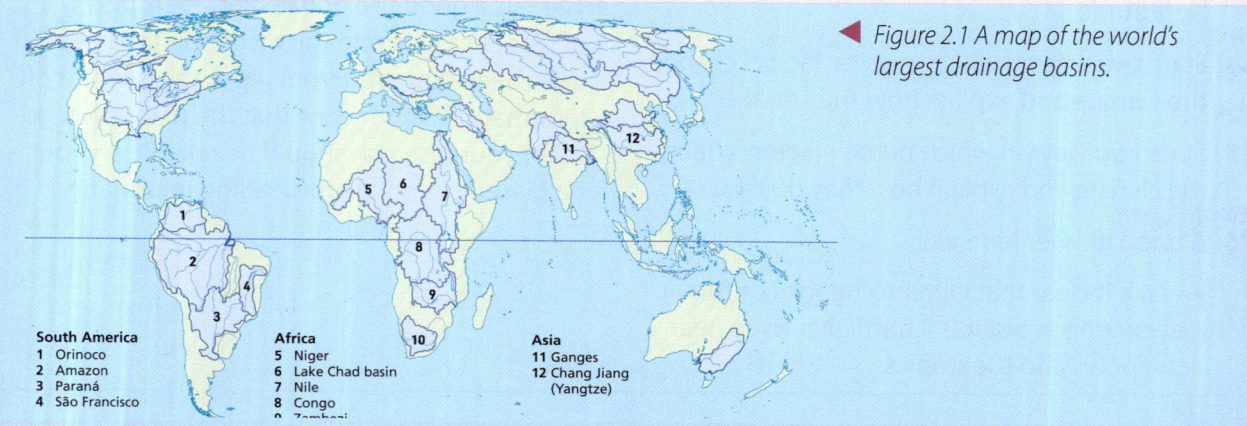

Figure 2.1 A map of the world's largest drainage basins.

**South America**
1 Orinoco
2 Amazon
3 Paraná
4 São Francisco

**Africa**
5 Niger
6 Lake Chad basin
7 Nile
8 Congo
9 Zambezi

**Asia**
11 Ganges
12 Chang Jiang (Yangtze)

## 2 How might climate change affect drainage basins?

## Where are you going?

While you look at climate change on a global level, your local drainage basin will be explored, along with a range of real-world examples, such as the Ganges River Basin. You will also look at flooding in the UK, and Dhaka in Bangladesh. You will explore the impact of drought and salination in Australia and drought management strategies in Singapore.

▲ Figure 2.2 Map of the world showing the locations of India, Bangladesh, Australia, the UK and Singapore.

▲ Figure 2.3 Drought conditions in Australia.

▲ Figure 2.4 Flooding in Dhaka, Bangladesh.

## Where does our water come from and where does it go?

This chapter explores how climate change is impacting the water systems in our environment. You will learn about drainage basins, which are areas where water collects and flows to a single point. You will also learn how rising temperatures are changing rainfall patterns, causing more floods and droughts.

### Discuss

1 How have you noticed the climate changing in your local area?
2 How might increased flood risk affect where people choose to live?
3 How might a severe drought affect your daily life?

# 2.1 What are drainage basins and what is climate change?

In order to understand how climate change might affect **drainage basins**, you need to understand what a drainage basin is, and how it functions. You must also understand what climate change looks like in terms of the volume of water entering a drainage basin.

## What is a drainage basin?

Imagine you are in your bathroom at home. You turn on the tap, cup your hands and splash your face with water. After the water hits your face, where does it go?

Hopefully, most of it falls back into the sink, flows into the plughole and down the drain. Now swap the water bouncing off your face for rain coming down from the clouds, swap the rim of the sink for mountain tops and the sink bowl for valleys, and you have a real drainage basin.

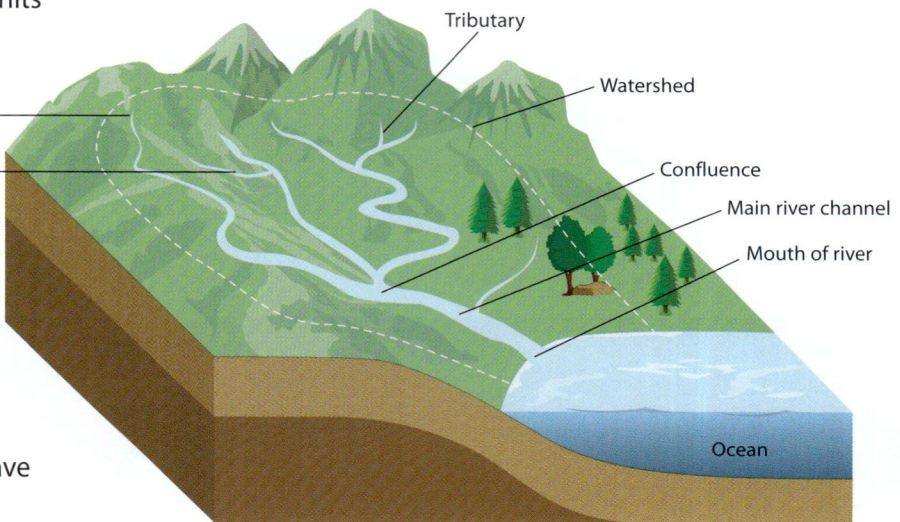

▲ Figure 2.5 The structure of a drainage basin.

A drainage basin is an area of land where all surface water flows to a single point, such as a river, lake or ocean. All the water that falls within its edges flows towards the lowest point. Precipitation that falls on one side of a mountain will flow into one drainage basin and precipitation falling on the other side of the mountain will flow into a different drainage basin. The top of the mountain is the boundary between these drainage basins and is called a **watershed**.

The water cycle is a continuous process that moves water around our planet. Heat from the Sun causes some of the water in oceans, rivers and lakes to evaporate (turn into vapour). Plants also release water vapour through transpiration. As all this vapour rises, it cools and condensation occurs,

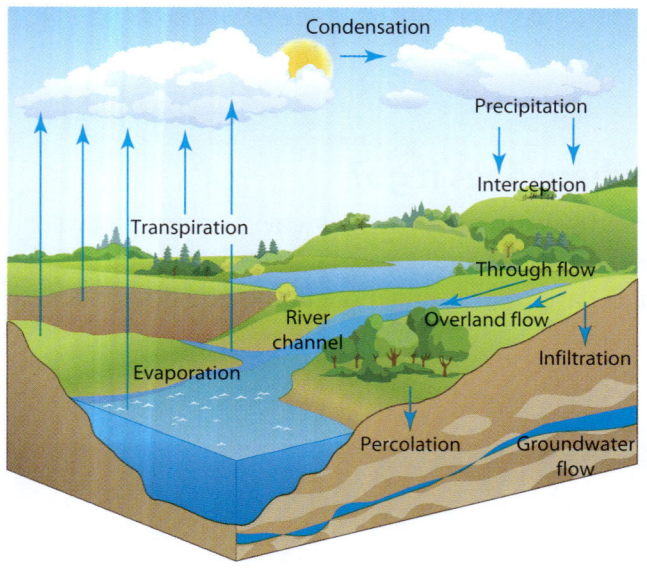

▲ Figure 2.6 A diagram showing the water cycle.

## 2 How might climate change affect drainage basins?

creating clouds. When the clouds get heavy, they release water as precipitation (rain, snow, hail or sleet). Some precipitation is intercepted by trees. Some flows across the land as surface run-off into rivers. The rest of the water infiltrates the soil. Some will move through the soil into the rock below by a process called percolation. Water underground returns to the sea, lakes and rivers via the process of groundwater.

## Climate change

As you learned in Chapter 1, climate change refers to long-term shifts in global weather patterns and average temperatures. It is as if the weather in your town suddenly started getting hotter and stormier year after year.

The Earth's average temperature has increased by about 1 °C since pre-industrial times (1850). This warming is mainly caused by human activities, especially burning fossil fuels (coal, oil and natural gas) and wood. Climate change affects sea levels and ecosystems around the world.

*Figure 2.7 Burning fossil fuels for energy has caused global temperatures to rise.*

### Key terms

**Drainage basin**: An area of land where all surface water flows to a single point, such as a river, lake or ocean.

**Tributary**: A smaller stream or river that flows into a larger river.

**Watershed**: The boundary between two drainage basins.

### Activities

1 Draw your own drainage basin. Use different colours to show highlands, **tributaries** and the main river.

2 What are the possible impacts on vegetation and humans if a drainage basin receives more precipitation than usual?

3 How have you noticed the climate changing in your local area?

## 2.2 How does climate change affect water systems?

Climate change has a big impact on **water systems**. It can cause more intense rainfall, longer dry periods, warmer temperatures and rising sea levels.

### How climate change impacts water systems

All of the impacts listed above directly affect drainage basins. For example, more intense rainfall can lead to drainage basins experiencing more flooding. On the other hand, longer dry periods could mean less water in rivers and streams within the basin. Understanding how climate change affects water systems in general can help you predict and prepare for the specific ways it might change your local drainage basins.

Climate change affects water systems in four main ways, as shown in Table 2.1.

| Factor | What happens | Result | Example |
|---|---|---|---|
| 1. More intense rainfall | Rainstorms become heavier and more frequent | Increased flooding in many areas | 2021: Germany experienced severe floods due to heavy rainfall |
| 2. Longer dry periods | Some regions get less rain for longer periods | More frequent and severe **droughts** | California has faced several long-lasting droughts in recent years |
| 3. Warmer temperatures | The air gets hotter | More water evaporates from lakes, rivers and soil | Lake Chad in Africa has shrunk dramatically due to increased **evaporation** (see Figure 2.8) |
| 4. Rising sea levels (see Figure 2.9) | Ocean water expands as it warms, and ice melts from glaciers | Coastal flooding and **erosion** increase | The Maldives, a country of low-lying islands, is at risk of disappearing under water |

▲ Table 2.1 How climate change affects water systems.

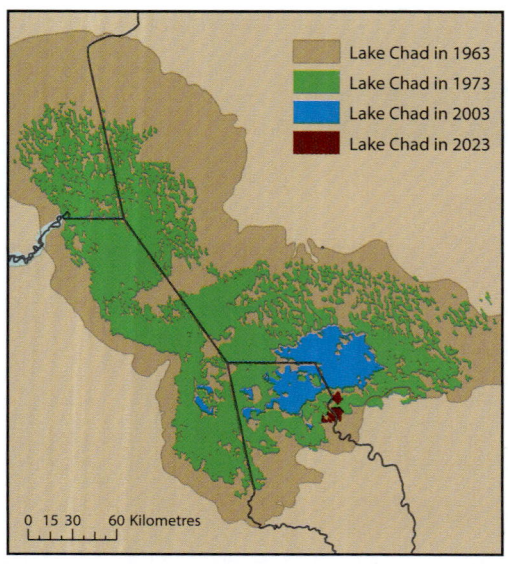

2024

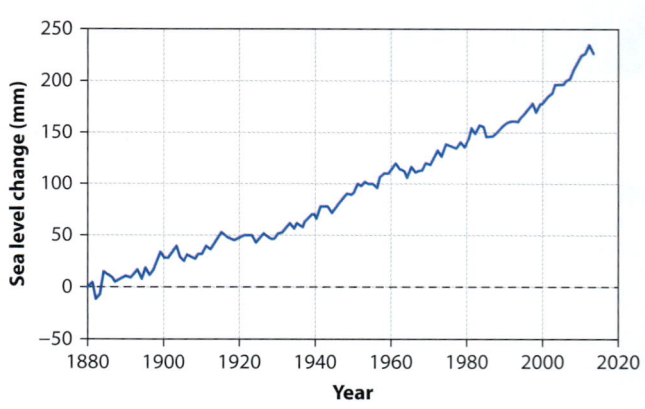

◀ Figure 2.8 Lake Chad has shrunk dramatically over 60 years.

▲ Figure 2.9 A graph showing the rise in sea levels over 140 years.

## 2 How might climate change affect drainage basins?

This matters because water is essential for all life on Earth. Changes in water systems affect:

- the water we drink
- the food we grow
- the homes we live in
- the animals and plants around us.

### How climate change affects a river basin

The Ganges river basin, located in India and Bangladesh, is one of the world's largest river systems. It supports over 400 million people – more than the entire **population** of the United States.

Climate change is affecting the Ganges water system in several ways:

- The yearly rainy season (monsoon) is becoming more intense, causing flooding. Homes, farms and businesses are being destroyed, and people are being put in danger.

- Ice in the Himalaya mountains is melting faster, resulting in changes in water supply throughout the year. In the short term this might mean more water is available, but in the long term there will be less water as glaciers shrink and do not reform.

- Rising sea levels mean the ocean is creeping higher, causing coastal areas to be flooded more often. This means that people are being displaced, having to abandon their homes to move to higher ground.

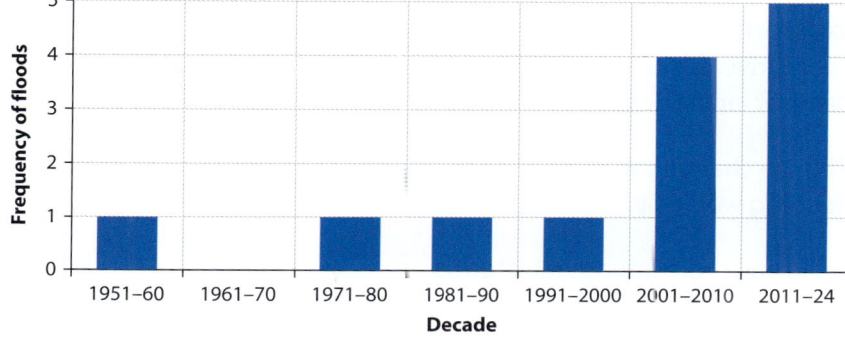

▲ Figure 2.10 A bar chart of severe flood frequency in Germany.

### Key terms

**Drought**: A period of unusually dry weather that lasts long enough to cause problems such as crop damage and/or water supply shortages.

**Erosion**: The wearing away of land by water, wind or ice.

**Evaporation**: When liquid water turns into water vapour (gas).

**Population**: The total number of people living in an area.

**Water systems**: Networks of water bodies like rivers, lakes and oceans.

### Activities

1. Look at Figure 2.10, which shows a bar chart of flood frequency in Germany. Write a short paragraph describing what trend you see in the chart. Why do you think this trend is happening?

2. Imagine you are a water droplet going through the water cycle. How might your journey be different now compared with 100 years ago due to climate change? Use the water cycle diagram in Figure 2.6 and at least **two** key terms from the lesson in your answer.

3. The Ganges river basin is facing three main challenges due to climate change. Choose one of these challenges and explain how it might affect the daily life of someone living in that area. Think about things like their home, food or job.

## 2.3 What are the causes and effects of flooding?

Climate change can cause more heavy rain and storms. Drainage basins can fill up too quickly and cause flooding. So, flooding due to climate change can affect the environment and people living near drainage basins.

### Causes of flooding

Flooding occurs when water overflows onto normally dry land. It can happen for many reasons, for example: heavy rainfall, melting snow and ice, **storm surges** from the ocean, river blockages (like dams or landslides).

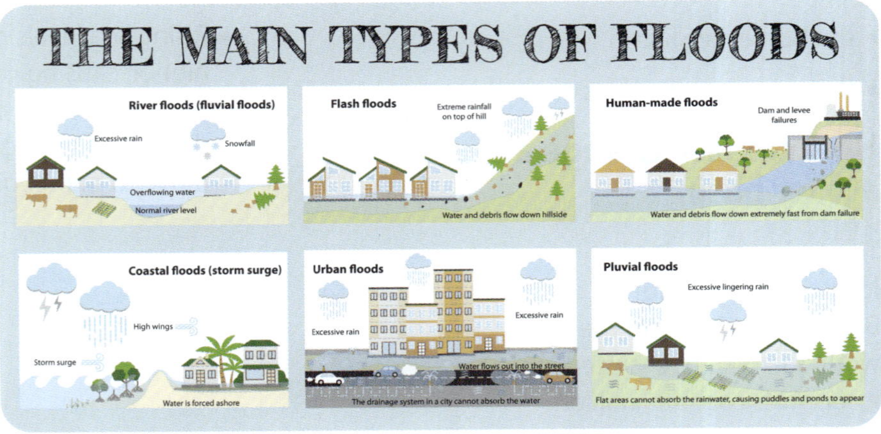

Climate change can make flooding worse by:

- causing more intense rainstorms
- melting snow and ice faster
- causing sea levels to rise.

▲ Figure 2.11 The six main types of flood.

### Impacts of flooding

Floods can have serious consequences, as shown in Table 2.2.

| Environmental impacts | Social impacts | Economic impacts |
| --- | --- | --- |
| Soil erosion | Damage to homes and businesses | Costly damage to infrastructure |
| Water pollution | Disruption to transportation | Loss of crops and livestock |
| Habitat destruction | Health risks from contaminated water | Decreased tourism |

▲ Table 2.2 Consequences of flooding.

In the winter of 2015–16, the UK experienced severe flooding. Storm Desmond caused record-breaking rainfall in Cumbria, leading to widespread flooding. There was a wide range of impacts, such as:

- over £1.6 billion in damages
- railway lines disrupted
- power outages affecting thousands
- thousands evacuated from homes
- riverbank erosion
- significant agricultural losses (crops and livestock)
- roads and bridges damaged or submerged
- thousands of homes and businesses flooded
- contamination of water supplies
- disruption to local ecosystems
- increased stress and anxiety among affected populations
- schools closed, disrupting education.

## 2 How might climate change affect drainage basins?

Figure 2.12 Fields flooded in the 2015–16 floods in the UK.

## Analysing a hydrograph

A **hydrograph** is a graph that shows how much water is flowing in a river over time (measured from a fixed point). It is a useful tool for understanding and predicting floods. Using your knowledge of the water cycle and drainage basins, you will know that precipitation (shown as bars on Figure 2.13) can take time to reach a river. The time it takes between the maximum rainfall and the maximum amount of water being in the river is known as **lag time**. The purple line on the graph shows the amount of water flowing through the river at a particular time of day (time is shown on the x-axis). As the amount of water in the river increases, the line goes up – this is known as the rising limb. The highest point the line reaches on the graph is known as **peak discharge**. As water moves through the river into a sea or lake (and assuming there is no more rainfall), the amount of water in the river will decrease, shown by the purple line on the graph going down – this is called the falling limb.

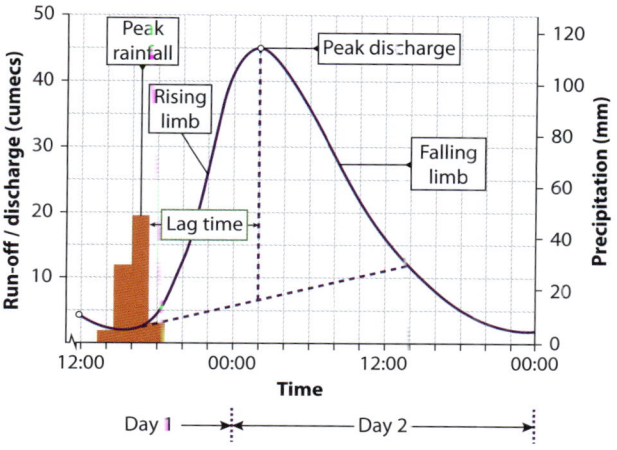

Figure 2.13 A storm hydrograph.

### Key terms

**Hydrograph**: A graph showing the discharge of a river over time.

**Lag time**: The time between peak rainfall and peak **river discharge**.

**Peak discharge**: The maximum discharge recorded on a hydrograph.

**River discharge**: The volume of water flowing through a river channel at any given point.

**Storm surge**: A rise in sea level caused by a storm.

### Activities

1 Use the storm hydrograph to answer the following questions:
   a On what day and at what time did rainfall reach its peak?
   b On what day and at what time was the river at peak discharge?
   c What was the total lag time between peak rainfall and peak discharge?

2 Why is there a lag time between rain falling and the river filling up and flooding its banks?

3 What strategies could be introduced to slow the speed at which rainwater enters rivers, in order to reduce the risk of flooding? Explain how your strategies would be effective. Discuss how increased flood risk might affect where people choose to live.

## 2.4 To what extent does climate change increase flood risk?

Think of a drainage basin as a giant sink, towards which all the water in an area flows. When we talk about **flood risk** increasing, we are really talking about that sink overflowing more often. Climate change can make this happen by causing more rain to fall, or snow to melt faster, filling up the sink more quickly than usual.

### How climate change increases flood risk

The city of Dhaka in Bangladesh has two of the world's biggest rivers flowing through it: the Ganges and the Brahmaputra. Dhaka faces severe flooding challenges due to a combination of factors intensified by climate change. Increased temperatures mean the warmer air holds more moisture, resulting in heavy downpours that can overwhelm the drainage basins. Warmer springs lead to the rapid melting of glaciers in the Himalayas, swelling rivers that flood surrounding areas. Rising sea levels are another critical issue, as coastal flooding becomes more frequent and severe, affecting low-lying regions of the city. Changing weather patterns have resulted in longer monsoon seasons, increasing the likelihood of destructive floods. For example, in July 2021, Dhaka experienced severe flooding after heavy rains coincided with high river levels, displacing thousands of people and highlighting the need for effective flood management strategies in the face of climate change.

▲ *Figure 2.14 How does climate change make flooding in Dhaka more likely?*

## 2 How might climate change affect drainage basins?

▲ Figure 2.15 The location of Dhaka, Bangladesh.

### Key term

**Flood risk**: The chance or possibility of an area being covered with water that is not usually there.

### Activities

1. Think about the 'giant sink' analogy for a drainage basin. List **two** ways in which climate change makes this sink more likely to overflow.

2. Dhaka, Bangladesh faces severe flooding issues. Name the two rivers that flow through the city and explain one way climate change is making flooding worse there.

3. Look at Figure 2.15 showing the location of Bangladesh. Discuss why you think Dhaka's position makes it especially vulnerable to flooding. Consider its location relative to mountains and the sea.

31

# 2.5 What are the causes and effects of drought?

Drought is a period of unusually dry weather that lasts long enough to cause problems like crop damage and water supply shortages. It is like when you are really thirsty, but there is no water around.

## Types of drought

Droughts happen when there is not enough rain for a long time. In a drainage basin, this means less water in rivers and lakes. As the Earth gets warmer due to climate change, some places might get less rain than usual, leading to more frequent and severe droughts. This can change how water moves through the drainage basin, affecting plants, animals and people who depend on that water.

▲ Figure 2.16 A photograph showing how drought affects soil. If there is not enough moisture in the soil, crops cannot grow.

There are different types of drought:

- meteorological drought, when there is less rainfall than normal
- agricultural drought, when there is not enough soil moisture for crops
- hydrological drought, when water levels are low in rivers, lakes and groundwater
- socioeconomic drought, when water shortages affect people and the economy.

## Causes of drought

Droughts can be caused by lack of rainfall, high temperatures increasing evaporation, changes in weather patterns (like El Niño) and human activities (such as overuse of water).

Climate change can make droughts worse by:

- causing higher temperatures, which increase evaporation
- changing rainfall patterns
- melting glaciers that supply water to rivers.

## Impacts of drought

Droughts can have far-reaching environmental, economic and social impacts, as shown in Table 2.3.

| Environmental impacts: | Social impacts: | Economic impacts: |
|---|---|---|
| - dried-up rivers and lakes<br>- loss of wildlife<br>- increased risk of wildfires<br>- **desertification**. | - water shortages for drinking and sanitation<br>- food shortages due to crop failures<br>- migration of people from drought-affected areas. | - reduced agricultural production<br>- higher food prices<br>- job losses in farming communities. |

▲ Table 2.3 Environmental, social and economic impacts of droughts.

## 2 How might climate change affect drainage basins?

▲ Figure 2.17 The characteristics of desertification.

Australia's Millennium Drought (1997–2009) was one of the worst droughts in Australia's history, affecting most of southern Australia, including parts of New South Wales, Victoria, South Australia and Western Australia. It caused major rivers like the Murray and Darling to have very low water levels. It made it hard for farmers to grow wheat, rice and other crops, with some areas experiencing desertification. This **water scarcity** led to strict water restrictions in big cities like Melbourne and Adelaide. It hurt native animal species like kangaroos and koalas, due to loss of **habitat** and food sources, and reduced the number of indigenous gum trees.

◀ Figure 2.18 The environmental, social and economic impacts of drought.

### Key terms

**Desertification**: The process by which fertile land becomes desert, typically as a result of drought, deforestation or inappropriate agriculture.

**Habitat**: The natural environment where a plant or animal lives.

**Water scarcity**: A lack of sufficient water resources to meet the demands of water usage in a region.

### Activities

1. How might a severe drought affect your daily life?
2. **a** Look at Figure 2.16. What does it show?
   **b** What do you think it would be like to live there if you were a farmer?
   **c** What might have caused this?
3. Study the selection of images in Figure 2.18.
   **a** Identify which one(s) are environmental impacts, which are social impacts and which are economic impacts.
   **b** Write your own caption for each of the images, describing what each shows.

## 2.6 In what ways can drought management strategies mitigate climate change?

When you learn about ways to manage drought, you are also learning how to help drainage basins cope with climate change.

### Ways to manage droughts

Saving water and using it more efficiently can help keep rivers and lakes from drying up during hot, dry periods. Planting trees and other plants that do not need much water can help stop soil from washing away when it does rain. Smart drought management also protects our drainage basins from some of the harmful effects of climate change.

### How do countries conserve water?

The Millennium Drought in Australia, which you learned about in the previous lesson, taught us that there are many ways to manage and **mitigate** drought, including:

- water **conservation**: using less water in homes, **agriculture** and industry
- improving **irrigation** efficiency: using techniques like drip irrigation
- water recycling: treating and reusing wastewater
- building reservoirs: storing water for dry periods
- drought-resistant crops: planting crops that need less water.

▲ Figure 2.19 Planting trees as part of the Great Green Wall project to reverse the desertification process in the Sahel.

Singapore has little fresh water of its own, so it has developed innovative ways to manage water:

- Catchment areas cover two thirds of Singapore's land surface.
- NEWater reclaims high-grade wastewater.
- Desalination plants turn seawater into drinking water.

▲ Figure 2.20 Singapore has water catchment areas and desalination plants as part of its water management strategy.

## Drought management strategies in the Sahel region of Africa

The Sahel is a dry region in Africa that stretches across several countries, including Senegal, Mali, Niger and Chad. This area faces frequent droughts, which can last for months or even years. Table 2.4 shows some ways people in the Sahel manage water scarcity.

These methods help communities of the Sahel cope with drought and protect their precious water **resources**. By using these strategies, people in the Sahel are working hard to slow, or even reverse the process of desertification, successfully adapting to the challenges in one of the world's toughest environments.

▲ Figure 2.21 Communities in the Sahel share wells and boreholes.

| Technique | Example |
|---|---|
| Water conservation | People in villages collect rainwater in large tanks during the short rainy season |
| Drought-resistant crops of the Sahel | Growing pearl millet and sorghum, which are traditional Sahelian grains that need less water |
| Livestock management in Sahelian communities | Reducing herd sizes during severe droughts to conserve water and protect grazing lands |
| Community action in Sahel villages | Sharing wells and boreholes among neighbouring villages to ensure everyone has access to water |
| Traditional Sahelian water-finding techniques | Using knowledge passed down through generations to find underground water sources |

▲ Table 2.4 Some of the ways people in the Sahel manage water scarcity.

### Key terms

**Agriculture**: The practice of cultivating soil, growing crops and raising animals for food, fibre and other products.

**Conservation**: Taking care of nature and protecting plants, animals and their habitats to keep them safe and healthy.

**Irrigation**: The provision of extra water to supplement rainfall to enable crops to be grown.

**Mitigate**: Reduce the impact of something.

**Resource**: Anything that people see as useful or valuable.

### Activities

1. Identify **three** methods used to manage drought in the Sahel region of Africa.
2. Explain how planting drought-resistant crops can help communities in the Sahel region cope with water scarcity.
3. Discuss the effectiveness of Singapore's water management strategies, such as NEWater and desalination, in addressing its limited freshwater resources compared with traditional methods used in the Sahel region.

# 2.7 What is salination and how is it affected by climate change?

As the Earth gets warmer, water evaporates faster, leaving salt behind. Also, rising sea levels can push salty ocean water into freshwater areas, making them saltier. Too much salt is harmful to plants and animals, and can make the water less suitable for drinking and farming.

## Understanding salination

**Salination** means an increase in the concentration of salt in soil or water. Imagine leaving a glass of saltwater in the sun – as the water evaporates, the salt stays behind. Salination can occur due to:

1. natural **weathering** of rocks that contain salt
2. irrigation using salty water
3. sea-level rise in coastal areas.

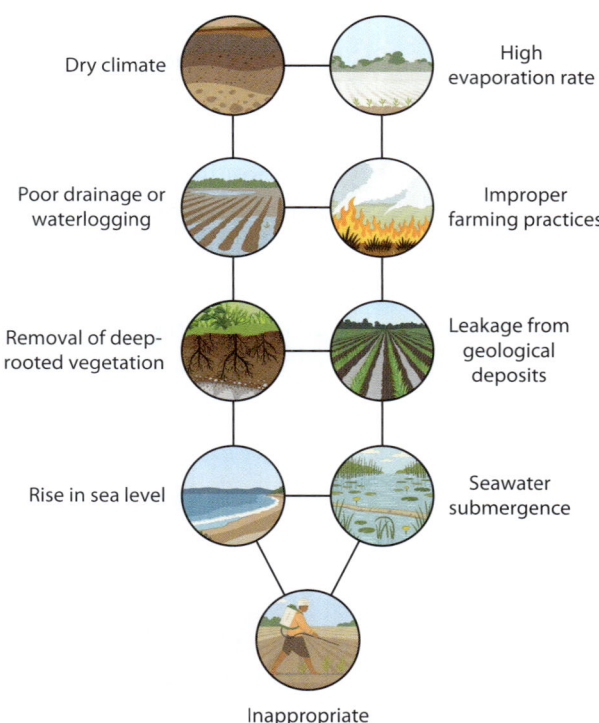

▲ Figure 2.22 The causes of salination.

As temperatures rise, water evaporates more quickly, leaving behind salt and making it more concentrated. This is harmful to fish and other animals that need clean water to survive.

## Effects of salination on drainage basins

Salination can affect drainage basins and the plants, animals and humans that live in them. An increased concentration of salt in **fresh water** makes it less suitable for drinking. Many plants cannot grow well in salty soil, meaning farmers' **crop yields** decrease. Salty soils can also be washed away more easily during heavy rainstorms. Some plants and animals are unable to **adapt** to the increased concentration of salt and may die, resulting in a loss of **biodiversity**.

The Murray–Darling Basin in Australia faces serious salination problems. Human activities, like clearing land for farms and using too much water for irrigation, have caused this issue. With less vegetation, more salt can build up in the soil, making it hard for crops to grow.

Despite the challenges of salination, some communities take advantage of salination techniques to extract salt for sale. For example, in Peru and Vietnam, people create salt ponds where seawater is collected and allowed to evaporate. As

▲ Figure 2.23 The effects of salination in the Murray–Darling Basin in Australia. There are very few plants that can grow on salt-affected land. The quality of grassland for farm animals is reduced enormously by rising salination.

## 2 How might climate change affect drainage basins?

the water evaporates, salt crystals form and can be harvested. This not only provides a valuable resource for local economies, but also demonstrates how communities can turn a challenge into an opportunity by using traditional methods to produce salt for cooking and other purposes.

To help reduce the effects of salination, there are some smart strategies that can be used:

- Special watering techniques, such as drip irrigation, give plants just the right amount of water without wasting it and help to prevent salt from building up in the soil.
- Farmers can grow salt-tolerant crops that can survive in salty conditions, which helps keep their farms productive.
- Restoring natural areas, such as wetlands, can help clean water and soak up extra salt.

Teaching farmers and communities about these solutions is essential for fighting salination. As climate change continues to affect our world, taking these steps will be important for keeping our drainage basins healthy and supporting the people who rely on them.

▲ Figure 2.24 Salt ponds in Vietnam.

▲ Figure 2.25 Effect of salinity on a mustard field.

### Key terms

**Adapt**: Change to meet a situation.

**Biodiversity**: The variety of different plants, animals and other living things in an area, which helps keep ecosystems healthy.

**Crop yields**: How much is produced from an area of land.

**Fresh water**: Found in rivers, lakes, ice sheets and precipitation, it is suitable for drinking.

**Salination**: The process of salt building up in soil or water.

**Weathering**: The process of breaking down rocks into smaller pieces by factors like wind, water, temperature changes and biological activity.

### Activities

1. Identify **three** causes of salination in drainage basins.
2. Explain how rising temperatures due to climate change can affect water quality due to salination.
3. Discuss how communities can turn the challenge of salination into an opportunity, using examples from countries like Peru and Vietnam.
4. a Look Figure 2.25. What does it show?
   b How does this affect plant life?
   c Where else in the world might this be happening, and why?

# 2.8 How can you use mapping and GIS to study drainage basins?

**GIS**, or **Geographic Information Systems**, is computer software that combines digital maps and information to help people solve current problems and make plans for the future.

## How do we use GIS for drainage basins?

GIS can be a useful tool for studying drainage basins, as it can create maps that show how areas might change over time, especially due to climate change. For example, if it rains more in a particular drainage basin, GIS can help you see where flooding might happen. If there is less snow, it can show you where rivers might dry up in the summer.

GIS helps us to map areas in order to see the size and shape of drainage basins. It enables geographers and town planners to see easily how high or low the land is, to help understand water flow. GIS can also show where water moves and where it is likely to collect. This information can be used to know where, and where not, to construct buildings. GIS helps people watch how land-use changes affect water availability. It also enables scientists to predict where flooding might occur.

## Layers in GIS

GIS uses different layers to organise information:

- Base map layer: shows streets and landmarks.
- Hydrology layer: displays rivers, lakes and wetlands.
- Land-use layer: illustrates how land is used, like farms or cities.
- Soil layer: shows different types of soil.
- Elevation layer: indicates how steep the land is.
- Transportation layer: displays roads and railways.
- Population layer: shows where people live.

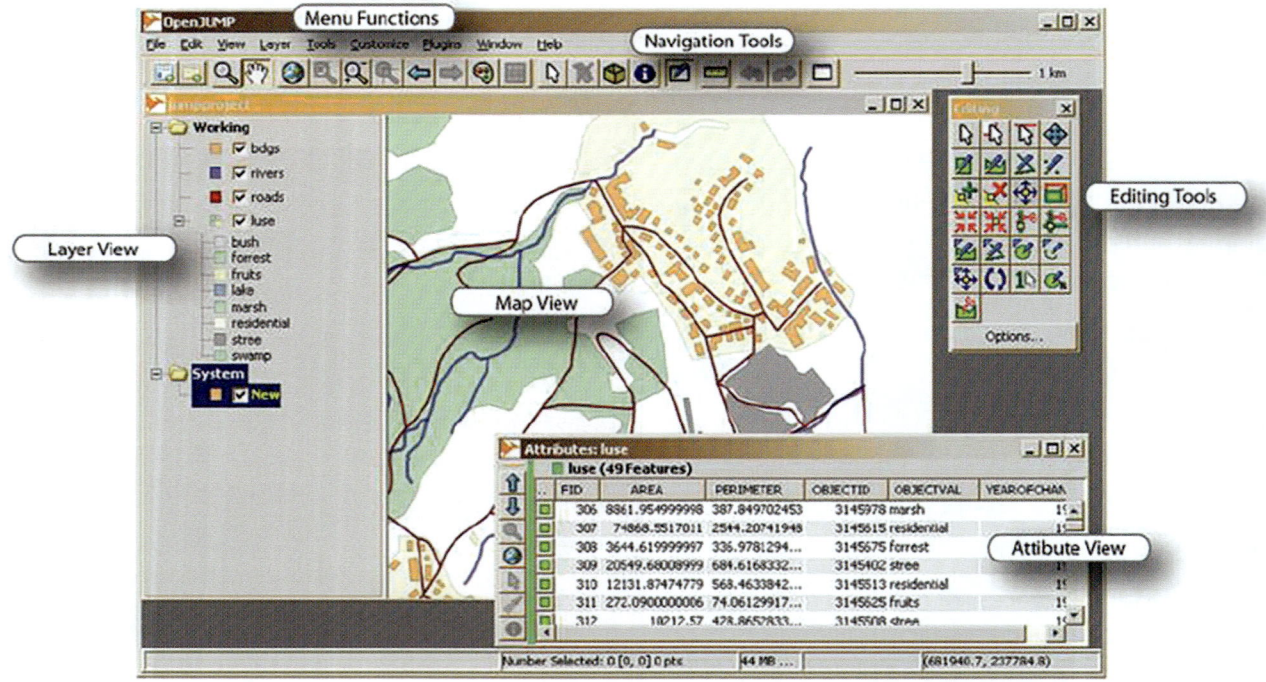

▲ Figure 2.26 GIS and its layers.

## 2 How might climate change affect drainage basins?

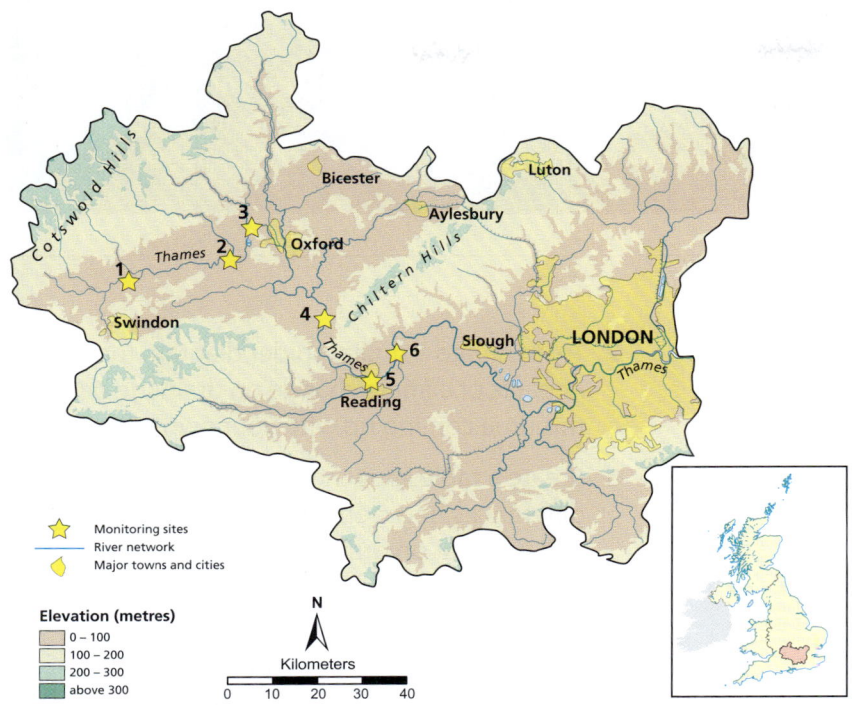

▲ Figure 2.27 A GIS-generated map of the Thames River Basin in the UK.

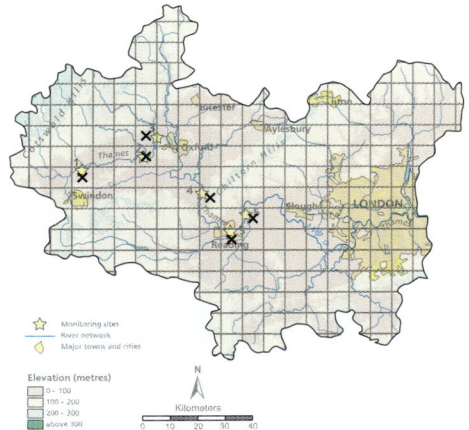

▲ Figure 2.28 A simple GIS map can be created by layering tracing paper over a map and drawing a grid on it.

### Key term

**Geographic Information Systems (GIS):** Think of GIS as a powerful computer tool that helps to create and analyse maps. It has many 'layers' of information, allowing us to see different aspects of the land, like water flow and land use.

### Activities

1. Create a simple GIS map:
    a. Use tracing paper and coloured pencils.
    b. Trace a base map of your area.
    c. On separate sheets, draw features like rivers and parks.
    d. On a third sheet draw roads and railways.
    e. On a fourth sheet draw some of the buildings and your school.
    f. Stack the sheets to create a layered map.

2. How does layering different types of information change what you learn from a map?

3. What other information would help you understand your local area better?

# 2 End-of-chapter tasks

## Reflection

Climate change can significantly impact drainage basins by altering rainfall patterns and increasing temperatures. This may lead to more flooding or droughts, affecting water availability for people, animals and plants. How can you predict and prepare for these changes to protect resources?

## Revision tasks

1 Create a spider diagram for drainage basins. Use the following stems:
   - Definition
   - Components (for example, rivers, lakes)
   - Importance
   - Human impact
   - Climate change effects
   - Management strategies

2 Try to create a similar spider diagram for the impacts of climate change on drainage basins, this time coming up with your own stems.

3 Create a table showing the similarities and differences between the impacts of flooding and drought on drainage basins. Use the same headings as your spider diagram for comparison.

## End-of-chapter review A

1 Study the climate graph for the Ganges River Basin in Figure 2.29. **Describe** the climate. (3 marks)

2 Figure 2.30 shows the location of the Ganges River Basin. **Describe** the location. (2 marks)

3 **Explain** how climate change is affecting water availability in the Ganges River Basin. (4 marks)

4 Figure 2.4, from Lesson 2.3, shows flooding in Dhaka, Bangladesh. **Explain** how flooding impacts daily life in the area. (4 marks)

5 **Discuss** the effectiveness of water management strategies in Singapore for combating drought. (4 marks)

6 **To what extent** is climate change a threat to drainage basins worldwide? (8 marks)

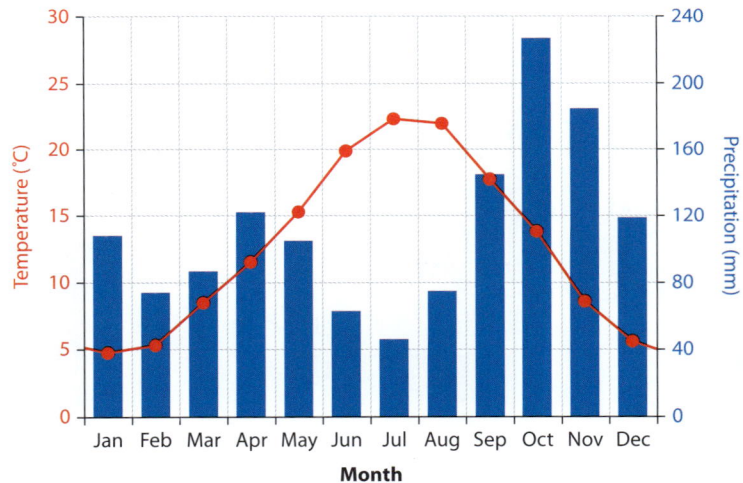

▲ Figure 2.29 Climate graph for the Ganges River Basin.

**2** How might climate change affect drainage basins?

▲ Figure 2.30 The location of the Ganges River Basin.

## End-of-chapter review B

Write a report comparing your local drainage basin and its impact on people to the Ganges River Basin. Your report should include the following sections:

- What is your local climate like, and how does it impact the landscape? How is this different from the Ganges River Basin?
- How do plants and animals adapt to your local environment? Why do they adapt differently in the Ganges River Basin?
- How does your local climate affect people? What are the advantages and disadvantages?
- How will climate change affect your local drainage basin and the people who live there?
- Overall, does your local drainage basin present more or fewer challenges and opportunities than the Ganges River Basin?

## 2 How might climate change affect drainage basins?

### End-of-chapter review support

### End-of-chapter review A

1. Include details about temperature and precipitation patterns throughout the year. Mention seasonal changes, such as the monsoon season, and provide specific data points (for example, average temperatures and rainfall amounts).

2. Provide geographical context by mentioning the countries it spans (India and Bangladesh), its major cities and significant geographical features (for example, proximity to the Himalayas and the Bay of Bengal). Use directional terms (for example, north and south) to clarify its position.

3. Identify at least two specific impacts of climate change, such as increased flooding due to heavier rainfall or reduced water supply from melting glaciers. Explain how these changes affect local ecosystems and human communities.

4. Discuss various effects, such as damage to homes and infrastructure, disruptions to transportation and health risks from contaminated water. Provide examples of how these impacts affect livelihoods, such as agriculture and local economies.

5. Evaluate specific strategies, such as water recycling (NEWater) and desalination. Discuss how these methods have successfully increased water supply and reduced dependency on external sources. Consider any challenges or potential drawbacks.

6. Present a balanced argument by discussing both the threats posed by climate change (for example, increased flooding, droughts and salination) and potential adaptive measures (for example, improved water management). Use specific examples from various drainage basins to illustrate your points and reach a well-supported conclusion.

### End-of-chapter review B

A good report will:

- focus on direct comparison
- include specific details about the local environment
- justify conclusions about potential future impacts of climate change, drawing from previous chapters
- include effective use of key geographical terms.

# 3 Why does the Lake District look different from the Himalayas?

## Chapter overview

### Why are you studying this?

The Lake District in England and the Himalayas (also known as Himalaya) in Asia look very different from each other because of their unique geological histories, climate conditions and human influences. By comparing these two landscapes, you can learn how different factors shape the Earth's surface over time. You will explore how rock types, weathering processes and the power of water create distinct features in each region. Understanding these differences helps you appreciate the diversity of Earth's landscapes and how they affect the people living here.

### Skills

In this chapter, you will learn about:
- geological processes like weathering, erosion and tectonic activity, and how landforms and ecosystems are created and shaped
- interpreting climate and biodiversity data, and using maps to show ecosystems, human activities and local landscapes
- comparing different landscapes and ecosystems, looking for similarities, differences and patterns in both physical and human geography
- how people adapt to different environments, assess environmental impacts and evaluate sustainable practices
- developing solutions to environmental challenges, researching conservation efforts and designing awareness campaigns to promote landscape preservation.

### Learning outcomes

By the end of this chapter, you will understand:
- how physical processes like weathering, erosion, glaciation and tectonic activity shape different landscapes
- the main similarities and differences between the Lake District and the Himalayas, including their size, age, height, climate, ecosystems and human activity
- how climate and geography influence the types of plants and animals that can live in each region
- how humans adapt to and impact these environments, and the challenges they face in living there
- the importance of conservation and sustainability in protecting unique landscapes for the future.

## What are the connections?

In Chapter 1, you learned about climate change, which plays a role in shaping landscapes over time. In Chapter 2, you learned how water moves through the environment via drainage basins. The Lake District has a cool, wet climate. It rains a lot there, and the rain collects in valleys, forming beautiful lakes. The Himalayas are still growing! Two giant pieces of Earth's crust are pushing against each other, forcing the land upwards. This process, called plate tectonics, is part of how Earth's systems shape and sculpt the land, creating mountains, shaping valleys and driving long-term changes in climate, ecosystems and human activities. You will learn more about this next year in Chapters 1 and 2 of *Discover Geography 8*. By comparing these two very different landscapes, you can see how climate, water and geological processes work together to shape our world. This will help as you move into Chapter 4, where you will learn about how plants and animals adapt to these diverse environments.

# 3 Why does the Lake District look different from the Himalayas?

## Where are you going?

This chapter focuses on two main areas: the Lake District – a hilly region in northwest England known for its lakes, forests and mountains, and the Himalayas – the world's highest mountain range, stretching across several countries in Asia.

▲ Figure 3.1 A map of the world showing the Himalayas, separating the Indian subcontinent from the rest of Asia, and the Lake District, in the UK.

## How do landscapes form, change and inspire us?

In this chapter, you will compare the gentle hills and lakes of the Lake District with the towering peaks of the Himalayas. You will learn how different types of rocks form these landscapes and how water, ice and weather shape them over millions of years. You will also explore how people have changed these environments and how the landscapes affect the way people live. By the end of this chapter, you will understand why different parts of the world can look so different from each other.

◀ Figure 3.2 A U-shaped valley in the Lake District – ancient volcanic and sedimentary rocks carved out by glacial erosion during the Ice Age.

▲ Figure 3.3 The (relatively) young, folded mountains of the Himalayas, formed by the collision of tectonic plates.

### Discuss

1. What are some differences you notice between the Lake District and the Himalayas just by looking at pictures?
2. How do you think the weather might be different in these two places?
3. If you lived in the Lake District or the Himalayas, how might your daily life be affected by the landscape?
4. Can you think of any ways that humans have changed the landscape in your local area?

# 3.1 How do landscapes form and change over time?

In this lesson, you will explore the processes that shape and transform **landscapes** over time, focusing on the distinct features of the Lake District and the Himalayas. By examining the geological forces, climatic conditions and human activities that contribute to the formation of these two diverse regions, you will gain a deeper understanding of how landscapes evolve. You will investigate how weathering, erosion and **plate tectonics** create unique landforms, helping you answer the question of why the Lake District and Himalayas appear so different.

## What forces have influenced the shape of the land?

### Internal forces

**Plate tectonics**: the Earth's crust is divided into huge plates that move slowly. When these plates collide, they can create mountains such as the Himalayas.

**Volcanic activity**: volcanoes can build new landforms and change existing ones.

### External forces

**Weathering**: this is when rocks are broken down by wind, water, temperature changes and living things.

**Erosion**: once rocks are broken down, they can be carried away by wind, water or ice.

**Deposition**: the broken-down rock is eventually dropped somewhere else, building up new landforms.

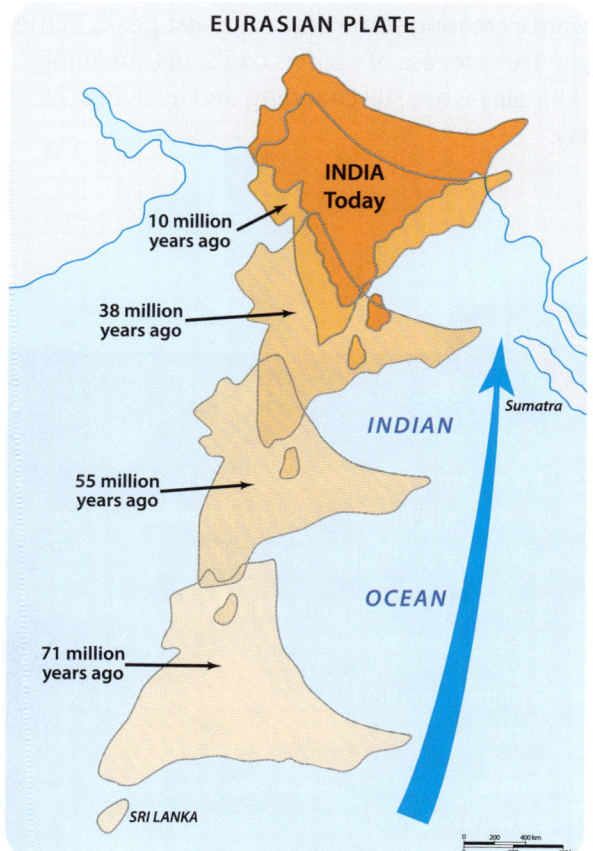

▲ Figure 3.4 The slow movement northward of the Indian plate toward the Eurasian plate.

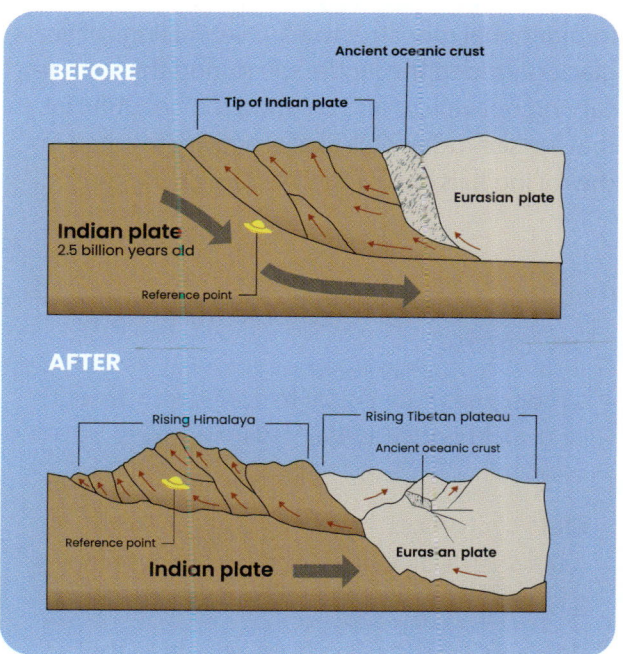

▲ Figure 3.5 The plate boundary of the Indian and Eurasian plates. Although they moved together slowly, the force is so strong that land is folded upwards, creating the Himalayas mountain range.

### 3 Why does the Lake District look different from the Himalayas?

a)

b)

▲ Figure 3.6 The impacts of a) erosion (a tree-shaped landform formed by rainwater erosion on the surface of the Xinjiang Plateau in China), and b) volcanoes (Mount Kelimutu, Flores, Indonesia) on the shape of landscapes.

The Lake District and the Himalayas have both been shaped by natural forces, but they exhibit distinct features due to their different formation processes and time scales. The Lake District, located in England, was primarily formed by ancient **volcanic activity**, which created its foundational rock structures. Over millions of years, glaciers eroded the landscape during the Ice Ages, carving out valleys and creating the beautiful lakes that we see today. This glacial activity resulted in the rolling hills and rugged terrain characteristic of the region. In contrast, the Himalayas are much younger in geological terms and are still actively forming. This majestic mountain range is the result of the ongoing collision between the Indian and Eurasian tectonic plates (see Figure 3.5). As these plates push against each other, they force the land upwards, creating some of the highest peaks in the world. This process of uplift is continual, meaning the Himalayas are still changing and evolving today.

#### Key terms

**Landscapes:** The visible features of an area of land, including mountains, valleys, rivers and lakes.

**Plate tectonics:** The theory that the Earth's outer shell is divided into several plates that glide over the semi-fluid layer beneath.

**Volcanic activity:** Processes related to the movement of molten rock from beneath the Earth's crust to the surface, leading to the formation of volcanoes.

#### Activities

1. Identify **two** processes that shape landscapes.
2. Draw a simple picture showing how weathering and erosion change landscapes. Label the parts of your drawing.
3. Describe how tectonic activity can change the Earth's surface.
4. Explain how glaciation has shaped the Lake District.
5. Evaluate whether glaciation or tectonic activity has had the greater impact on shaping landscapes, using examples from the Lake District and the Himalayas.

## 3.2 What are the main differences and similarities between the Lake District and the Himalayas?

By comparing the size, height, age and ecosystems of the Lake District and the Himalayas, and how they were shaped by natural forces like glaciers, you can see both the connections and contrasts between them. In this lesson you will also think about how these regions are affected by human activities (including tourism) and climate change.

## Similarities

### Reason for shape

Both the Lake District and the Himalayas were shaped by glaciers during the Ice Ages. Glaciers are huge masses of ice that move slowly over land, carving out valleys and creating unique landforms. This process left behind features like lakes and valleys in the Lake District and helped form the rugged terrain of the Himalayas.

### Ecosystems

Both regions have diverse ecosystems that support a variety of plants and animals. In the Lake District, you can find species like red deer, red squirrels and various birds, while the Himalayas are home to animals like snow leopards and diverse plant life, including rhododendrons. Each ecosystem is specially adapted to its physical environment. (See Figure 3.7.)

### Tourism

Both the Lake District and the Himalayas are popular tourist destinations. People visit the Lake District for its beautiful hiking trails and stunning lakes, while the Himalayas attract adventurers and climbers, especially those who want to hike to the base of Mount Everest. Tourism in both places offers opportunities for outdoor activities.

### Sustainability

Both regions face environmental challenges due to human activity and climate change. Issues like **pollution**, deforestation and climate change

a)  b)

▲ Figure 3.7 Different wildlife that can be spotted in the Himalayas (a) and the Lake District (b).

threaten their ecosystems. It is important for visitors and locals to work together to protect these beautiful landscapes for future generations.

## Differences

### Size and scale

The Lake District is a small area located in northwest England, covering about 2362 square kilometres. In contrast, the Himalayas are a massive mountain range that stretches across several countries, measuring approximately 2400 kilometres long. This difference in size makes the Himalayas one of the largest mountain ranges in the world.

### Height

The highest peak in the Lake District is Scafell Pike, which stands at 978 metres. In comparison, the Himalayas boast Mount Everest, the tallest mountain in the world, reaching a height of 8848 metres. This significant difference in height illustrates the dramatic scale of the Himalayas. (See Figures 3.8, 3.9 and 3.10.)

## 3 Why does the Lake District look different from the Himalayas?

▲ Figure 3.8 The rolling hills and valleys of England's Lake District, showing elevations below 1000 metres.

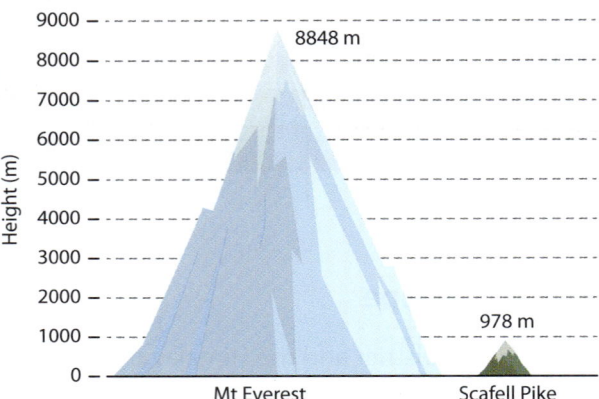

▲ Figure 3.10 The Himalayas dwarfing the Lake District. How many Scafell Pikes could you fit on top of each other to make one Mt Everest?

▲ Figure 3.9 The dramatic peaks and deep valleys of the Himalayas, with Mount Everest reaching 8848 metres.

## Climate

The climate in the Lake District is mild and wet, with cool summers and mild winters, which supports its lush greenery. The Himalayas, on the other hand, have a climate that varies greatly. It can be tropical at the base but becomes cold with permanent snow and ice at the peaks. This range of climates influences the types of plants and animals found in each region.

## Age

The Lake District was formed about 450 million years ago, making it an ancient landscape. The Himalayas, however, are much younger, having started to form around 50 million years ago. This difference in age affects their geological features and appearance.

### Key terms

**Pollution:** The contamination of the environment.

**Sustainability:** The ability to maintain ecological balance by protecting natural resources and the environment, ensuring they can be used by future generations.

### Activities

1. Identify the location of the Lake District and the Himalayas (write down both the continent and country/countries).
2. Create a Venn diagram to show what is the same and what is different about the Lake District and the Himalayas. Write at least **two** things in each section.
3. Explain how climate differs between the Lake District and the Himalayas.
4. Compare the two landscapes in terms of physical and human geography. Which differences are most significant? Explain why.

## 3.3 How do climate and geography influence the plants and animals in each region?

By examining the different climates (the mild, wet climate of the Lake District and the varied climate of the Himalayas), you can understand how these conditions shape ecosystems. In this lesson, you will learn how geography and climate create different habitats. Understanding these connections will help you appreciate the diversity of life in both regions and highlights the importance of protecting these ecosystems.

## Lake District

The climate in the Lake District is cool, wet and mild all year round. This region's relief is known for its rolling hills and valleys containing beautiful lakes. The plants here include deciduous trees like oak and ash, which thrive in the lower areas. As you climb higher, you will find heather and grasslands. In the damp areas, moss and lichen grow, adding to the lush greenery.

The Lake District is home to many animals. In the woodlands, you can spot red squirrels and badgers. The pastures are filled with sheep and cattle, while ospreys and water birds can be seen around the lakes. These animals have adapted to live in this cool and wet environment, making the Lake District a vibrant ecosystem.

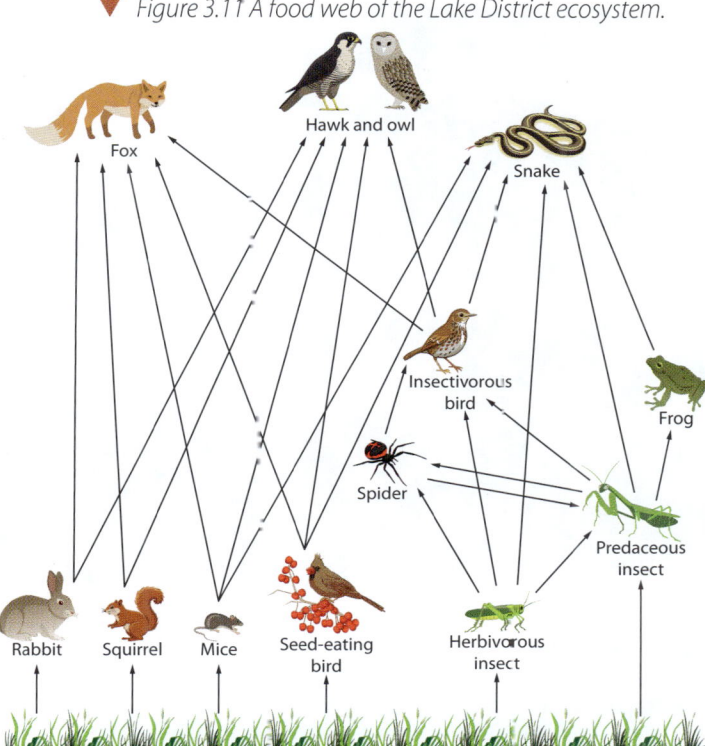

▼ Figure 3.11 A food web of the Lake District ecosystem.

## Himalayas

In contrast, the Himalayas have a climate that varies greatly with altitude. (We learned in Chapter 1 how temperature and oxygen decrease with altitude.) The relief here features towering mountains, deep valleys and high plateaus. At lower altitudes, you will find tropical forests filled with diverse plants. Moving up, the landscape changes to pine and fir forests at middle elevations. Above the treeline, alpine meadows flourish, while only lichens and mosses survive at the highest points.

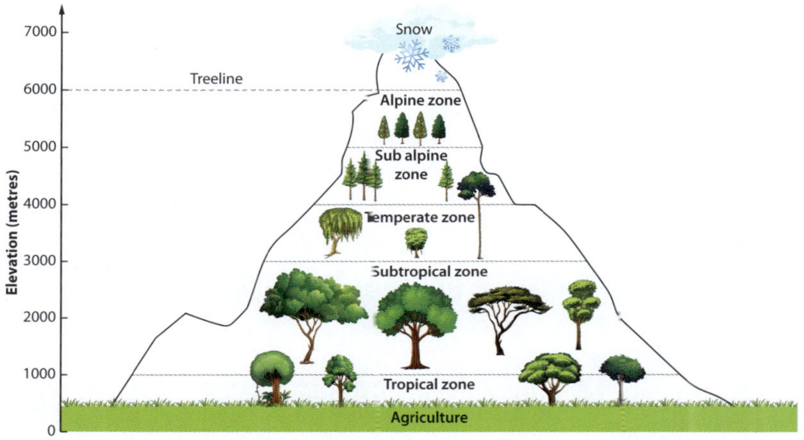

▲ Figure 3.12 Vegetation zones in the Himalayan region. How does plant life change with altitude in the Himalayas?

## 3 Why does the Lake District look different from the Himalayas?

The Himalayas also host a variety of animals. In the lowland jungles, you can find tigers and elephants. As you go higher, snow leopards and mountain goats roam the rugged terrain, and yaks are commonly seen on the high plateaus. These animals have special **adaptations** to survive in their harsh environments.

In both the Lake District and the Himalayas, plants and animals have adapted to their specific surroundings, showcasing the incredible diversity of life on our planet.

◂ Figure 3.13 a) Himalayan marmot: Thick fur and a fat layer that provide insulation against the cold temperatures.
b) Turkmenian markhor goat: Has long, twisted horns and strong hooves, enabling it to navigate the steep, rocky terrains.
c) Peregrine falcon: Exceptional speed and amazing eyesight, allowing it to hunt effectively from high altitudes during its rapid dives.
d) Red squirrel: The bushy tail aids in balance and serves as a parachute during jumps, helping it manoeuvre skilfully through the trees.

### Key terms

**Adaptation**: A change made to meet a situation.

**Insulation**: A covering that prevents heat loss.

### Activities

1. Create a climate graph for the Lake District. Include temperature as a line graph and rainfall as a bar chart.

| Month | Jan | Feb | Mar | Apr | May | Jun | Jul | Aug | Sep | Oct | Nov | Dec |
|---|---|---|---|---|---|---|---|---|---|---|---|---|
| Temp (°C) | 2 | 3 | 4 | 7 | 9 | 12 | 14 | 13 | 12 | 9 | 6 | 4 |
| Rainfall (mm) | 150 | 120 | 100 | 80 | 90 | 100 | 110 | 120 | 110 | 130 | 130 | 150 |

2. Describe how one plant or animal in the Lake District is adapted to its environment.
3. Explain how altitude affects ecosystems in mountain environments.
4. Compare the ecosystems of the Lake District and the Himalayas. Evaluate which ecosystem is more vulnerable to climate change. Give reasons for your judgement.

# 3.4 How have humans adapted to live in these diverse landscapes?

In the Lake District, residents may engage in farming, tourism and outdoor activities that suit the mild, wet climate and rolling hills. In contrast, people living in the Himalayas have developed techniques for farming on steep slopes, and adapted their homes to withstand harsh weather conditions, including heavy snowfall. This lesson highlights the creativity and resilience of humans in response to geographical challenges. In this lesson, you will see the strong connection between humans and their environment, which emphasises the importance of respecting and protecting these diverse landscapes for future generations.

## Challenges and opportunities

### Lake District

In the Lake District, agriculture plays a vital role. For centuries, people have farmed sheep, which has significantly influenced the landscape. They have built stone walls to mark fields and manage grazing patterns, creating a distinctive rural scenery. The region's beautiful views attract many tourists, leading to a thriving tourism industry. Hotels, restaurants and outdoor activities provide jobs and boost the local economy. The abundant rainfall in the Lake District is also crucial. It is harnessed for **hydroelectric power** and provides water to nearby cities. This careful management of water resources shows how residents adapt to their environment while maximising its benefits.

▲ Figure 3.14 Sheep farming is a traditional way of using the natural resources in the Lake District.

### Himalayas

In contrast, the Himalayas present a different set of challenges. Here, **terraced farming** allows people to cultivate crops on steep mountainsides. These flat areas are essential for growing food in a region where flat land is scarce. Yaks are another vital part of life in the Himalayas. At high altitudes, yaks are used for transportation, as well as for food and clothing, making them indispensable to the local culture. The homes in the Himalayas are uniquely designed with thick walls and small windows to retain heat in the cold mountain climate.

▲ Figure 3.15 Farmers have adapted to the terrain in Nepal by creating terraces to grow rice.

# 3 Why does the Lake District look different from the Himalayas?

People living at high elevations have also adapted physically. They often develop larger lung capacities and more red blood cells to cope with the thinner air and lower oxygen levels. This adaptation is crucial for survival in such a challenging environment.

In both the Lake District and the Himalayas, traditional knowledge about local environments has been passed down through generations. This wisdom helps communities live in harmony with their surroundings, showcasing human **resilience** and adaptability in diverse landscapes. Understanding these adaptations deepens our appreciation of how geography shapes human life.

▲ Figure 3.16 Firewood found in the foothills of the Himalayas is carried up to the mountain villages, often by hand.

a)

b)

▲ Figure 3.17 Traditional stone and whitewashed houses in the Lake District (a), and wood or stone mountain houses in the Himalayas (b). Both use materials that are found in their environments.

## Key terms

**Hydroelectric power**: Electricity generated by harnessing the energy of flowing water, often through dams or turbines.

**Resilience**: The ability of a system to recover from shocks or setbacks.

**Terraced farming**: A method of growing crops on the side of a hill or mountain by creating flat areas (terraces) to prevent soil erosion.

## Activities

1. Identify one type of farming used in the Lake District.
2. Describe one way people in the Himalayas adapt their homes to the environment.
3. Explain how farming practices differ between the Lake District and the Himalayas.
4. Compare the Himalayas and the Lake District. Which environment poses greater challenges for human survival? Explain why.

## 3.5 What impact do human activities have on these environments?

In the Lake District, activities like tourism, farming and construction can lead to pollution, habitat loss and changes in the natural environment. Similarly, in the Himalayas, human activities such as deforestation, **overgrazing** and climate change can disrupt ecosystems and threaten local wildlife. By examining these impacts, you can see the importance of sustainable practices that protect both the Lake District and the Himalayas.

## Challenges caused by human activity

### Challenges in the Lake District

- **Agriculture**: Sheep farming has shaped the landscape for centuries, resulting in open grasslands, but potential **soil erosion** if not managed properly.
- **Tourism**: The Lake District attracts millions of visitors each year, which can lead to erosion on popular hiking trails and increased pollution from litter and waste. However, it also brings income and jobs to the area.
- **Water management**: Building reservoirs and dams has changed natural water flows, creating new lakes but disrupting local ecosystems.

### Challenges in the Himalayas

- **Deforestation**: Clearing forests for agriculture and fuel affects soil stability and reduces biodiversity.
- **Mining**: Extracting minerals leads to damaged landscapes and polluted water sources, harming wildlife and local communities.
- **Climate change**: Human-caused global warming is melting glaciers at an alarming rate, threatening water supplies for millions.

### Common challenges in both regions

- **Urbanisation**: Growing towns and cities **encroach** on natural areas, leading to habitat loss.
- **Pollution**: Air and water pollution negatively impacts ecosystems and the health of local wildlife.
- **Infrastructure development**: Roads, buildings and other structures alter natural habitats, making it harder for wildlife to thrive.

▲ Figure 3.18 Building dams and reservoirs in the Lake District disrupts local ecosystems.

▲ Figure 3.19 Environmental pollution in the Himalayan water of river Bagmati.

### 3 Why does the Lake District look different from the Himalayas?

## Positive human impacts in both the Lake District and the Himalayas

- **Conservation efforts**: Establishing protected areas and national parks helps preserve these beautiful landscapes.
- **Sustainable tourism**: Eco-friendly practices support local economies while minimising environmental damage.
- **Scientific research**: Studies in both regions contribute to our understanding of geology, ecology and climate change, providing insights for future conservation efforts.

Figure 3.20 Communities are making positive changes to combat the challenges, such as having plastic bottle collection points at Everest Base Camp. They have also replanted trees in the Lake District.

Understanding these impacts helps us recognise the importance of balancing human activities with environmental protection to ensure the health of these unique ecosystems for generations to come.

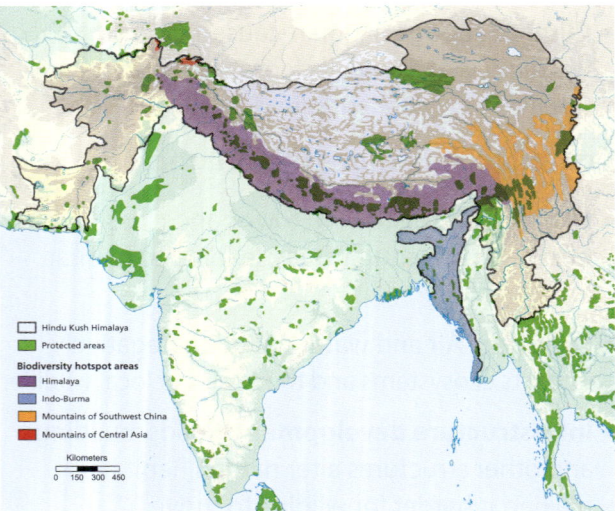

### Key terms

**Encroach**: To slowly move into or take over an area that is usually natural.

**Overgrazing**: When too many animals eat grass and plants in one area, which can damage the soil and reduce plant growth.

**Soil erosion**: The wearing away of the upper layer of soil, usually by water or wind.

**Sustainable tourism**: Travelling in a way that is good for the environment and helps local people, so that beautiful places can be enjoyed by future generations.

### Activities

1. Identify one human activity that has changed the Lake District.
2. Describe how tourism affects the natural environment in mountain regions.
3. Explain how deforestation in the Himalayas affects both people and ecosystems.
4. Create a two-column chart listing positive and negative human impacts on both the Lake District and the Himalayas. You can use symbols and sketches to illustrate your points.

## 3.6 How do these landscapes influence culture and daily life?

In this lesson, you will explore how the unique features of the Lake District and the Himalayas shape the cultures, lifestyles and traditions of the people who live in these regions. You will focus on aspects such as art, recreation and community practices that reflect the influence of these landscapes.

### Artistic inspiration

Both landscapes have inspired local artists, writers and musicians. The stunning scenery of the Lake District has led to a rich tradition of art and literature, with many artists capturing its beauty in paintings and poems. Similarly, the dramatic peaks of the Himalayas have influenced local crafts, including traditional textiles and paintings that depict the natural environment.

### Outdoor recreation

The geographical features of both regions promote various outdoor activities. In the Lake District, hiking, climbing and water sports are popular among locals and tourists alike. This love for outdoor recreation fosters a strong community spirit, as residents often participate in local events and festivals centred around these activities.

▲ Figure 3.22 Artwork inspired by the Lake District.

In the Himalayas, trekking and mountaineering are significant not only for adventure but also for promoting tourism. Local communities often organise trekking routes and provide services for visitors, which helps sustain their economy and preserve cultural practices.

### Community practices

Both regions showcase community practices influenced by their landscapes. In the Lake District, traditional sheep farming has shaped not only the landscape but also local customs and festivals celebrating agricultural heritage. Events such as sheepdog trials highlight the importance of farming in the community.

▲ Figure 3.23 A hiker in the Himalayas.

### 3 Why does the Lake District look different from the Himalayas?

In the Himalayas, traditional agricultural practices, such as terracing, have developed in response to the mountainous terrain. Community gatherings often revolve around seasonal agricultural activities, reinforcing social bonds and cultural identity.

## Environmental awareness

The distinctive features of these landscapes also promote a strong sense of environmental stewardship among local residents. In the Lake District, conservation initiatives, such as tree planting and habitat restoration, are common community activities. Residents often engage in efforts to protect local wildlife and promote sustainable tourism.

In the Himalayas, awareness of environmental issues, such as deforestation and glacial melting, has led to community-led conservation projects. Local organisations often work to educate residents and tourists about the importance of preserving their natural heritage.

▼ Figure 3.24 Sheep dog trials are an annual summer event in the Lake District, attracting many visitors.

▲ Figure 3.25 Local students learning about conservation in the Darjeeling Himalayan hill region.

### Key terms

**Artistic inspiration**: The influence of natural landscapes on creative expressions, including visual arts and literature.

**Community practices**: Traditions and customs that come from the unique culture of a region, often reflecting local livelihoods.

**Environmental awareness**: Recognising the importance of protecting natural resources and ecosystems.

**Outdoor recreation**: Activities that take place in natural environments promoting physical health and community engagement.

### Activities

1. Create a piece of art (drawing, painting or digital art) inspired by either the Lake District or the Himalayas. Write a short paragraph to explain how the landscape has influenced your work.
2. In what ways do outdoor recreational activities strengthen community ties in both regions?
3. How do traditional agricultural practices adapt to the geographical features of each landscape?
4. What role does environmental awareness play in the daily lives of people living in these regions?

# 3.7 What environmental challenges do these regions face, and how are they being addressed?

Both regions face challenges like climate change, pollution and habitat loss due to human activities. In the Lake District, efforts focus on sustainable tourism and conservation, while in the Himalayas, initiatives include **reforestation** and protecting endangered species.

## Challenges in the Lake District

The Lake District faces several environmental challenges. One major issue is overgrazing by sheep. When too many sheep graze in one area, they can damage the soil, leading to erosion and a loss of plant diversity. This means fewer plants can grow, which affects the entire ecosystem. Another problem is water pollution from agriculture and sewage, which can harm fish and other wildlife in the lakes. Additionally, tourism puts pressure on the landscape. With millions of visitors each year, paths become worn down, wildlife is disturbed and litter can spoil the natural beauty.

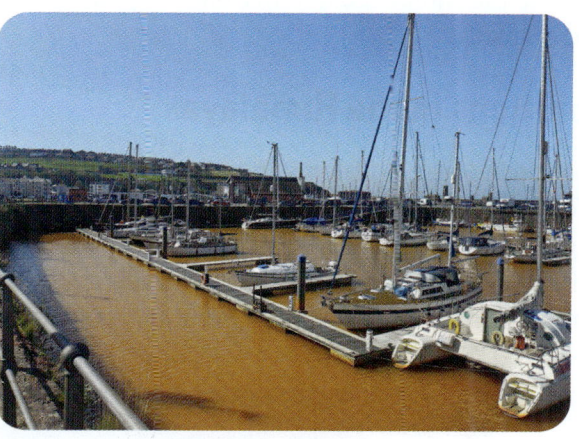

▲ *Figure 3.26 Whitehaven Harbour has been contaminated by run-off from the nearby coal mine and the construction of a railway tunnel.*

## Solutions in the Lake District

To tackle these challenges, several solutions are being implemented. Sustainable grazing practices encourage farmers to manage their sheep numbers better, allowing the land to recover. Reforestation projects help restore areas where trees have been cut down. Improved water treatment and regulations on agricultural run-off are essential for keeping lakes clean. Finally, visitor management strategies and educational programmes teach tourists how to protect the natural environment while they enjoy it.

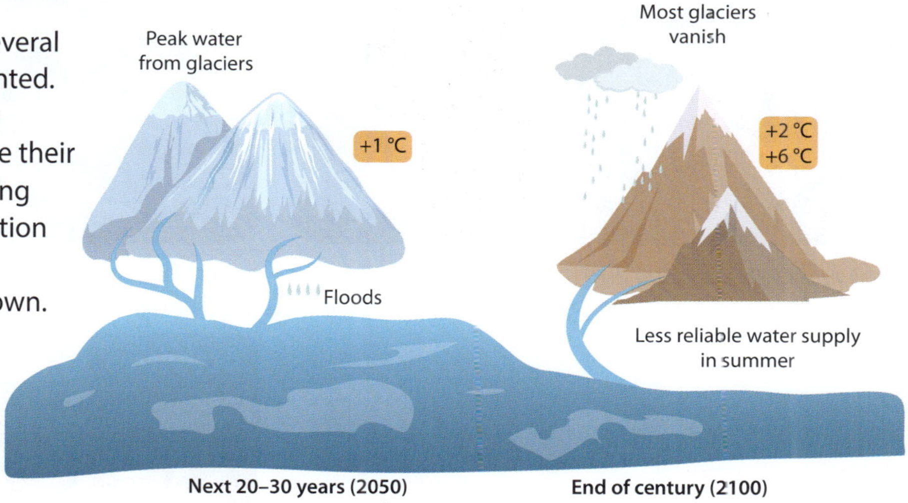

Peak water from glaciers
+1 °C
Floods
Most glaciers vanish
+2 °C
+6 °C
Less reliable water supply in summer
Next 20–30 years (2050)
Melting glaciers over the next 25 years will cause an increase in the amount of water flowing from the mountains, especially in summer, increasing flood risk lower down.
End of century (2100)
By the end of the century, many glaciers are likely to have vanished, meaning less water flowing into the rivers,

▲ *Figure 3.27 Glacier melt initially results in increased flood risk in areas at the bottom of the drainage basin, such as Dhaka, Bangladesh (as you saw in Chapter 2) and then water shortages when the glacier is gone.*

## Challenges in the Himalayas

The Himalayas also face significant environmental issues. Deforestation is a major concern, as trees are cleared for agriculture and fuel, leading

# 3 Why does the Lake District look different from the Himalayas?

to a loss of biodiversity. Melting glaciers due to climate change threaten water supplies for millions of people and cause flooding further downstream. In addition, air pollution affects the delicate mountain ecosystems, harming plants and animals.

## Solutions in the Himalayas

To address these problems, initiatives like reforestation programmes and the creation of protected areas are crucial for preserving habitats. International cooperation is needed to combat climate change, with countries working together to reduce greenhouse gas emissions. Promoting clean energy sources, such as solar and hydroelectric power, can help decrease pollution and reliance on fossil fuels.

## Common approaches

In both regions, community involvement is key. People are encouraged to participate in conservation efforts and support sustainable tourism initiatives. Scientific research also plays an important role in understanding and protecting these ecosystems, helping to develop effective solutions for the challenges they face.

a)

b)

▲ Figure 3.28 Stone paths in a) the Himalayas and b) the Lake District, which are popular trekking and hiking destinations, help protect against erosion. Bags of rocks are brought by helicopter to repair paths in the Lake District.

> **Activities**
>
> 1 Identify **one** environmental challenge facing the Himalayas.
>
> 2 Describe **one** threat to the Lake District environment.
>
> 3 Explain how climate change is affecting the landscapes of the Himalayas.
>
> 4 Design an infographic that summarises the main strategies used to manage environmental challenges in both regions. Include a paragraph stating which strategy you think is most effective. Explain why.

> **Key term**
>
> **Reforestation**: The process of planting trees in an area where forests have been cut down or damaged.

# 3.8 How can we appreciate and preserve diverse landscapes around the world?

This lesson encourages you to explore ways to appreciate natural beauty through activities like hiking, photography and learning about local cultures. It also discusses conservation efforts, sustainable practices, and the role of community involvement in preserving landscapes. By understanding how to care for these regions, you can become responsible stewards of the Earth and advocate for the protection of diverse environments globally.

## Education

Education is key. Learning about different landscapes, like mountains, forests and deserts, helps you understand their importance to local and global ecosystems. When you know how these places support plants, animals and people, you can appreciate them more.

## Responsible tourism

When visiting natural areas, practising **responsible tourism** is essential. Following 'Leave No Trace' principles means you should take only pictures and leave only footprints. This helps keep the environment clean and safe for wildlife. Supporting eco-friendly businesses also encourages sustainable practices that protect nature.

## Supporting conservation

Another way to help is to support conservation efforts. You can donate to or volunteer with organisations that work to protect landscapes. These groups often organise clean-up events or tree-planting days, which can be a fun way to make a difference.

## Reducing environmental impact

Make daily choices to reduce your impact on the environment. Simple actions, like using reusable bags or recycling, help combat climate change and reduce pollution. Every small effort counts!

## Spreading awareness

It is important to spread awareness about what you learn. Share information about landscapes and their challenges with friends and family. The more people know, the more likely they are to care and take action.

▲ Figure 3.29 The 'Leave No Trace' principles.

▲ Figure 3.30 A beach clean-up event.

## 3 Why does the Lake District look different from the Himalayas?

### Respecting local cultures

When visiting different places, you should respect local cultures. Learning about the traditions and beliefs of local communities helps us understand their connection to the land. This respect fosters positive relationships and encourages sustainable practices.

### Participating in citizen science

You can also join **citizen science** projects, which allow regular people to help with scientific research. This could be anything from counting birds to tracking weather patterns, contributing to our knowledge of ecosystems.

### Using social media responsibly

When sharing beautiful landscapes on social media, it is important to do so responsibly. Avoid geotagging sensitive areas to protect them from overcrowding.

### Supporting sustainable development

You can support sustainable development by encouraging policies that balance human needs with environmental protection. By appreciating and protecting local landscapes, we can ensure that future generations enjoy the beauty of our diverse planet.

▼ *Figure 3.31 A 100 per cent recyclable and reusable shopping bag.*

▲ *Figure 3.32 A Monarch butterfly is caught, recorded and released by a citizen scientist for the Monarch Watch project in Canada.*

> **Activities**
>
> 1. Identify **one** example of a conservation project.
> 2. Describe **one** way tourists can reduce their impact on landscapes.
> 3. Keep a journal for a week where you document your efforts to practise responsible tourism or conservation in your local area. Include illustrations and reflections on what you have learned about the importance of conservation.
> 4. Evaluate different approaches to preserving landscapes (for example, national parks, laws, sustainable tourism). Which do you think is most effective for long-term preservation? Why do you think this?

> **Key terms**
>
> **Citizen science**: Projects that allow regular people to help scientists collect data and conduct research, contributing to scientific knowledge.
>
> **Responsible tourism**: Travelling in a way that respects nature and local cultures, ensuring that our activities do not harm the environment.

# 3 End-of-chapter tasks

## Reflection

Landscapes around the world are constantly shaped by physical processes, climate and human activity. Why do you think it is important for geographers to study and compare different landscapes like the Lake District and the Himalayas?

## Revision tasks

1. Create a spider diagram to show the different physical processes that shape landscapes. Use the following stems:
   - Weathering
   - Erosion
   - Deposition
   - Tectonic activity
   - Glaciation

2. Create a table comparing the Lake District and the Himalayas. Include columns for:
   - Height above sea level in metres
   - Age
   - Climate
   - Ecosystems
   - Human activities

3. Draw and label a diagram to show how altitude affects plant and animal life in the Himalayas.

## End-of-chapter review A

1. Study the photographs of the Lake District and the Himalayas (Figures 3.2 and 3.3). **Describe** one difference in how the landscapes were formed. (2 marks)

2. Using Figure 3.10, **describe** how the heights of the Lake District and the Himalayas differ. (2 marks)

3. **Explain** how glaciation shaped the Lake District's landscape. (3 marks)

4. **Explain** how tectonic plate movement is still shaping the Himalayas today. (3 marks)

5. **Explain** two similarities between the ecosystems of the Lake District and the Himalayas. (4 marks)

6. **To what extent** have human activities had a positive or negative impact on these landscapes? (8 marks)

## End-of-chapter review B

Imagine you are writing an article for a travel and environment magazine called *World Landscapes*. The editor has asked you to explain why the Lake District and the Himalayas are both special but also under threat. Your article should include:

- a short introduction to both landscapes (location, main features)
- a comparison of how they were formed
- an explanation of how humans use and adapt to each landscape
- a discussion of the main environmental challenges facing each region
- a conclusion suggesting how both areas can be preserved for the future.

You can choose how to present your article – as a written piece with images, a poster, or even a recorded presentation.

## 3 Why does the Lake District look different from the Himalayas?

### End-of-chapter review support

#### End-of-chapter review A

1. Look closely at the diagrams. Focus on the processes shown (for example, volcanic, glacial, tectonic). Choose one clear difference and describe it in a short sentence.

2. Use the data in the figure to compare the tallest mountain in each region. Include both the names and the height values. Keep your answer brief but precise.

3. Think about the effects of glaciers during the Ice Age. Identify two or three landforms created by glaciation. Use geographical terms like 'valley', 'erosion' and 'deposition'.

4. Refer to the tectonic plates involved and the process they are causing. Show how this process is continuing and what effect it has on the mountains.

5. Choose two features the ecosystems share. For each one, explain how it is a similarity. Use examples of plants, animals or types of habitat to support your explanation.

6. Consider specific human activities, such as tourism, agriculture or conservation efforts. Discuss both the benefits and drawbacks these activities bring to the landscapes, and provide examples to illustrate your points.

#### End-of-chapter review B

A good response will:

- clearly compare the Lake District and Himalayas
- use geographical vocabulary such as glaciation, tectonics, ecosystem and sustainability
- include real examples of human activities and conservation efforts
- suggest realistic solutions for preserving these landscapes.

# 4 How does life adapt to its environment?

## Chapter overview

### Why are you studying this?
Geographers are interested in how the physical environment affects people. In this chapter you will explore how human and non-human life overcomes the challenges presented by extreme environments.

### Skills
In this chapter, you will learn about:
- climate graphs and how to interpret them
- line graphs and how to interpret them
- how to interpret photographs as a form of geographic data
- accurately describing location.

### Learning outcomes
By the end of this chapter, you will understand:
- how plants and animals adapt to the environment
- that people can overcome the challenges of living in extreme environments
- the variation in the extent of global warming
- the impacts that climate change will have on deserts.

## What are the connections?

In Chapter 1 you explored why climate varies. In this chapter you will see the effects of these variations.

This chapter will help you when you come to Chapter 6 and see how Russia is affected by its changing climate.

## Where are you going?

You will begin with a global view of biomes, before zooming in to consider how this looks in India, from the tropical forests to the deserts. You will then focus on India's Thar desert, followed by the people who live north of the Arctic Circle.

▲ Figure 4.1 Map of the world showing the location of the Arctic Circle and India.

# 4 How does life adapt to its environment?

## Opportunities and challenges

Any physical environment can create challenges which people adapt to as well as opportunities they take advantage of.

In the temperate climates of Western Europe, people might prepare themselves for the risk of flooding (see Chapter 2) but also have opportunities for farming.

In the Mediterranean areas of southern Europe there are challenges of wildfire during the hot, dry summers, but also opportunities for tourism, with people attracted by that same hot and dry weather.

▲ Figure 4.2 Temperate climates can support farming, but heavy rainfall can cause floods.

▲ Figure 4.3 Wildfires in Penteli, Greece (2023).

### Discuss

1. What is your local physical environment like? Can you describe the climate, landscape and vegetation?
2. Can you think of any advantages to living in your environment?
3. Does your local environment present any challenges? How do people adapt?

# 4.1 How does climate affect the world's biomes?

To understand how people adapt to their environment, you first need to know what these environments are. You also need to know where in the world these environments are found and why they are there.

## Variations in climate

The Sun's energy is more concentrated in some parts of the world than others. It is more concentrated closer to the equator and less concentrated as you move away. It is also concentrated in some places at different times of the year.

These differences in the Sun's energy mean that some places have higher temperatures than others, or have higher temperatures at different times of the year.

▼ Figure 4.4 The UK has cool winters and warm summers with rain all year round.

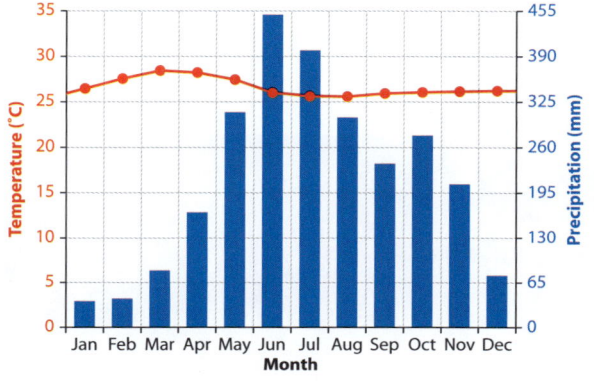

▲ Figure 4.5 Kerala has high temperatures all year with a lot of precipitation.

For example, in the United Kingdom, the average temperature in July is 20 °C, whereas in January it is 7 °C. This is a temperate climate.

In Kerala, in southern India, the temperature stays close to 26 °C throughout the year. This is a tropical climate.

## How climate affects the biome

The amount of the Sun's energy striking the Earth influences the physical environment in many ways, including affecting what grows there. Plants use energy from the Sun. In Kerala and other tropical areas, plants can grow all year. In the United Kingdom, there is not enough energy for them to grow during the winter.

As well as energy from the Sun, plants need water.

In Kerala, there is a dry season from December to March, but then lots of precipitation throughout the rest of the year.

In northern India, in the state of Rajasthan, there is still a high temperature all year (although more

▲ Figure 4.6 In Kerala, high rainfall and year-round energy from the Sun allow dense plant growth.

## 4 How does life adapt to its environment?

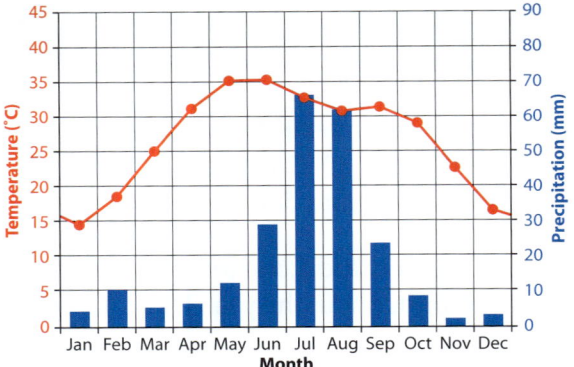

Figure 4.7 The temperature in Rajasthan stays high but there is very little precipitation.

country that it has several biomes, from the tropical rainforest biome of Kerala to the desert biome of Rajasthan (see Figure 4.9). Other places are dominated by just one biome. The temperate climate of the United Kingdom creates a deciduous woodland biome across most of the country.

Biomes slowly change from one to another. In India, the **dense** tropical rainforest is slowly replaced by more **sparsely** growing trees before becoming semi-arid scrubland and then desert.

▲ Figure 4.8 Low levels of rainfall mean that there is little vegetation in Rajasthan's Thar Desert.

of a temperature range), but there is much less precipitation. This means there is not enough water for many plants to grow, and plants do not grow to be very big.

These differences in climates create different **biomes**. Biomes are major habitats defined by their climate and vegetation. India is such a large

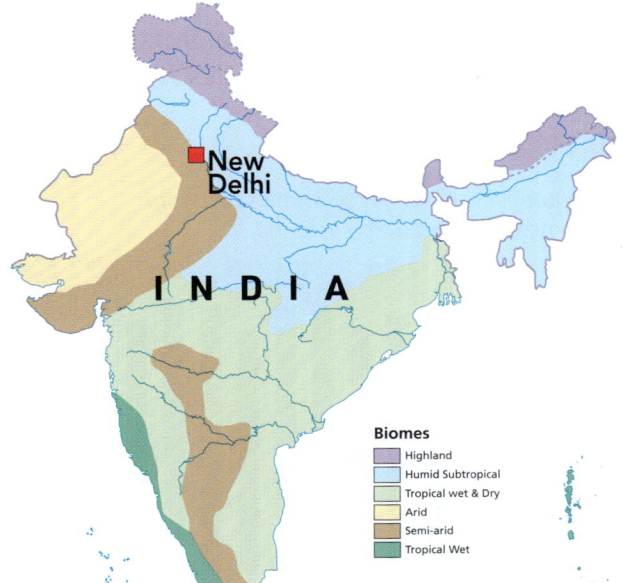

▲ Figure 4.9 India is such a large country that it has several biomes.

### Key terms

**Biome**: Areas of the planet with similar climate and vegetation.

**Dense**: Crowded.

**Sparse**: Spread out.

### Activities

1. Use Figure 4.5 to describe Kerala's climate.
2. Contrast Kerala's climate and Rajasthan's climate (shown in Figure 4.7).
3. Explain why the biome of Kerala is different from Rajasthan's.
4. Draw a diagram to show how vegetation changes as you move away from the equator.

## 4.2 What are the characteristics of hot desert biomes?

Life, in all its forms, needs water. When water is limited, such as in hot deserts, geographers can see how people make adaptations to overcome challenges and seize opportunities.

## Hot desert climate

Deserts can be defined as areas of the world that receive less than 250 mm of precipitation on average in one year. In hot desert areas, this low level of rainfall is combined with high temperatures (see Figure 4.7).

When it does rain, much of it evaporates back into the atmosphere. However, some will **percolate** through the weathered rock to be stored in **aquifers** deep below the surface.

Clear skies mean that the days are usually very hot. However, the temperature at night usually falls suddenly, making it very cold. Hot deserts can have a high temperature range across the year as well as across the day.

## Vegetation in hot deserts

Plants evolve to survive in their environment. In hot deserts, plants have had to adapt to the lack of water. Many plants do this by having long **tap roots** which reach down to aquifers. Water can be lost through the leaves of plants. As a result, plants in the hot desert usually have small leaves or no leaves at all.

The lack of water means that vegetation is sparse in hot deserts. This has an impact on the rest of the ecosystem.

▼ *Figure 4.10 Plants in the Thar Desert.*

# 4 How does life adapt to its environment?

Sun → Grass → Jird → Desert fox

▲ Figure 4.11 A food chain in the Thar Desert: grass absorbs energy from the Sun, which is transferred to the jird that eats the grass, which is transferred to the fox that eats the jird.

## Animals in hot deserts

Plants are the producers in an ecosystem. They can produce energy from sunlight. Animals rely on plants as an energy source that then moves through the food chain (see Figure 4.11).

The lack of plants in deserts such as the Thar means that there are also few animals.

The animals that live there must also adapt to the climate. Many, such as the jird, burrow into the ground to shelter from the sun during the day and come out to feed at night. The desert fox has large ears which help it locate its prey in its burrow and also allow it to lose body heat into the atmosphere.

▲ Figure 4.12 In the Thar Desert, rock has been weathered into sand.

## Landscapes in hot deserts

With little vegetation, the landscapes of hot deserts are often characterised by rocky outcrops that stand above either thin soil or sand. Sand is created by rocks that have been weathered by heat and wind.

### Key terms

**Aquifer**: Water stored in porous rock below the ground.

**Percolate**: Move down through faults or gaps in rock.

**Tap roots**: Long roots of plants that have evolved to reach water deep under the ground.

### Activities

1 Describe how the climate of hot deserts affects the landscape.

2 Study Figure 4.10. Explain how the plant shown there will have adapted to life in the hot desert.

3 Explain why animals in the Thar Desert would struggle if moved to a cold climate.

4 Explain why the Thar Desert is a difficult environment for life to adapt to.

# 4.3 How do people adapt to life in hot deserts?

Human societies are found in one form or another all over the world. This is possible because people either make changes to the environment, or they change to suit the environment

## Finding water

A lack of water is one reason why **population density** is often very low in desert areas. The people who do live there often adapt by finding alternatives to using water, such as cleaning pots and pans with sand.

The Thar Desert is the most densely populated desert in the world. Therefore, one adaption has been to change the environment and to bring in water from other regions that have higher rainfall. The Indira Gandhi Canal brings water 650 km north and is used to **irrigate** crops such as wheat and cotton.

## Farming in the desert

Before modern irrigation schemes, farmers in some areas of the Thar Desert relied on Khadeens.

▲ Figure 4.13 Irrigation makes large-scale farming possible even in hot deserts.

These are very low walls made from local stones that are laid out across an area to be farmed. When it rains, the low wall traps the water for long enough to allow it to soak into the ground and means that a crop can then be planted.

▲ Figure 4.14 Thick walls and few windows keeps out the heat of the sun.

# 4 How does life adapt to its environment?

## Houses in hot desert regions

Houses in hot deserts are often built with similar design principles. They often have thick walls and small windows (see Figure 4.14). This helps to keep the heat of the Sun out during the day and keep the warmth in during the cold nights.

It is expensive and difficult to bring building materials across the desert, so houses are usually made with local materials. This is often clay that has been baked hard by the Sun.

In desert towns such as Jaisalmer, houses are built from thick sandstone blocks, and around central courtyards to provide shade and cool air. Many modern houses have air conditioning, adapting the environment to make it more comfortable for the people who live there.

▲ Figure 4.15 Painting houses white helps to keep them cool.

### Key terms

**Irrigate**: Providing water for farming.

**Population density**: The number of people living in a given area.

### Activities

1. Describe how people have adapted to the hot desert environment.
2. Describe how people have changed the environment of the Thar Desert.
3. Suggest the problems that might arise from making changes to the Thar Desert, such as increasing the amount of farming or the population density.

# 4.4 What are the opportunities for people in hot deserts?

Sometimes, adaptation is about surviving. At other times, adaptations allow people to take advantage of the conditions a place offers and to thrive there.

## Mining in the hot desert

Mining for minerals at or below the surface of the Earth can be very disruptive. Opencast (surface) mining can use up large areas of land and often create both noise and air pollution. As population density is often very low in hot deserts, mining there causes much less disruption to people, which is why mining is more common there than in more densely populated areas.

In the Thar Desert, companies mine for minerals such as gypsum and phosphorite. In the part of the desert in Pakistan, there are also many coal mines. This coal provides a significant source of fuel for Pakistan's power stations.

## Tourism in the hot desert

There is a growing opportunity to make money in the tourism industry of the Thar Desert. People visit to see the unique wildlife found there, experience the extreme environment and visit sites such as the city of Jaipur, famous for its historic buildings. Many of these were painted pink in 1876 to welcome the future King of the United Kingdom, Edward VII, at a time when India was part of the British Empire.

▲ Figure 4.16 The desert may have space for mining, but it leaves a scar on the landscape.

## Conflict in the hot desert

Hot desert areas can feel like vast open spaces. This might lead to people thinking that they can **exploit** the resources there without consequences. However, because resources, especially water, are so limited, conflict can arise from competing demands.

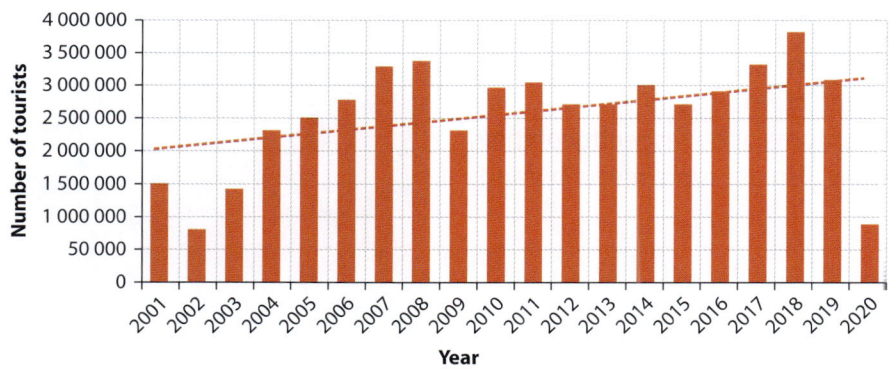

▲ Figure 4.17 A graph to show the number of foreign tourists visiting the desert region of Rajasthan.

## 4 How does life adapt to its environment?

▲ Figure 4.18 Tourists are attracted to Rajasthan's historic cities like Jaipur.

Increased farming means that more water is taken for irrigation. But this water is taken from ground water that is also taken up from wells for drinking. These wells are starting to run dry.

Opencast mining uses a lot of land. This is land that might have been used by farmers to graze their animals. Farmers often have to move their animals over large areas to find enough for them to eat as vegetation is so limited.

Although tourism can create jobs for local people, it can also cause conflict. Tourists might not understand local customs or be respectful of their way of life. They may also use more resources and create more waste.

### Key term

**Exploit**: Remove and use natural resources.

### Activities

1 Explain why mining takes places in the Thar Desert.

2 Figure 4.17 shows the number of foreign tourists travelling to the Thar Desert in Rajasthan. Describe the trend shown.

3 Suggest why fluctuating numbers of tourists might cause problems for the people of the Thar Desert.

4 Explain why there might be conflict between farmers and one other group that uses the Thar Desert.

5 Suggest how conflict might arise over resources in the area of the world where you live.

# 4.5 What are the characteristics of cold desert biomes?

Cold climates present challenges to life. Plants and animals evolve over time to meet the conditions found in this harsh environment. People use technology to overcome the challenges found there.

## Cold desert climate

Deserts are not defined by their temperature but by their lack of precipitation. Cold deserts, such as those in the Arctic Circle, get similar levels of precipitation (rain and snow) as hot deserts such as the Thar Desert.

Cold deserts often have a wide temperature range. Days are very short in the winter and there is very little energy from the Sun, so it is very cold. During the summer, days are very long and there is more energy from the Sun. It does not usually get very hot, but it is much warmer than the winter (see Figure 4.19).

## Vegetation in cold deserts

Vegetation tends to be sparse in cold deserts due to the lack of rainfall, the lack of sunlight for much of the year and the cold temperature that leaves the soil frozen and would damage the leaves of plants.

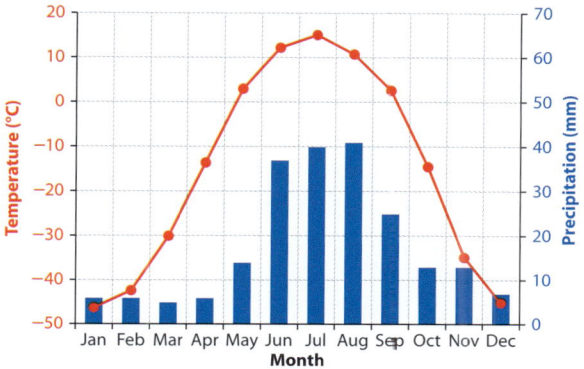

▲ Figure 4.19 A climate graph for Oymyakon, Russia.

Plants adapt to these conditions by growing close to the ground, away from the cold winds. Leaves tend to be small and waxy to limit water loss and protect them from the cold. Because most of the soil is permanently frozen, plants have shallow roots in the thin layer of soil that thaws each year. Many plants have evolved to grow and flower rapidly during the short summer, such as cotton grass in northern Canada (see Figure 4.20).

▲ Figure 4.20 Cotton grass growing in northern Canada.

# 4 How does life adapt to its environment?

▲ Figure 4.21 The Arctic fox (left) and desert fox (right) have adapted to their environments.

The seeds then fall to the ground to be frozen until the next year when they will germinate and grow, repeating the cycle.

## Animals in cold deserts

Animals need insulation against the cold. Some, like polar bears, grow thick fur to protect them, whereas marine animals like walruses have thick layers of fat called blubber, which provides insulation.

There is limited food during the long winters. Most arctic animals build up fat reserves during the summer, so they can survive with less food later in the year. Some animals, such as brown bears, hibernate during the winter.

Animals often have to travel long distances in search of food. Reindeer **migrate**, looking for enough vegetation to eat. Predators such as Arctic foxes turn white in winter, so they are camouflaged against the snow. Their prey, like the Arctic hare, do the same.

## Landscapes in cold deserts

The soil in cold deserts is often permanently frozen (called permafrost). Only the top layer of soil thaws during the warmer summer.

When snow and ice melt, the water cannot infiltrate the still-frozen soil and so it sits on the surface. This means that low-lying and flat areas of cold deserts may be covered in shallow pools of water during the summer. These pools of water provide breeding grounds for insects such as mosquitoes.

### Activities

1. Study Figure 4.19. Describe the climate of Oymyakon, Russia.
2. Describe how the climate of Oymyakon differs from that of Rajasthan (see Figure 4.7).
3. Describe how the climate of Oymyakon is similar to that of Rajasthan.
4. Explain the difference between plants in cold deserts and those in hot deserts.
5. Explain the differences in adaptations between the Arctic and desert fox (see Figure 4.21).

### Key term

**Migrate**: To move from one place to another.

# 4.6 How do people adapt to life in cold deserts?

Cold and dry conditions make life difficult for people in cold deserts, such as those who live inside the Arctic Circle. However, people adapt to these conditions either by using traditional methods that have been developed over generations or by using modern technological strategies.

## Food in cold deserts

Crops cannot usually be grown in cold deserts. The **indigenous people** of these regions survive by either herding animals or hunting them. For example, the Sami of Scandinavia (in northern Europe), rely on their herds of reindeer for meat and milk, and use their skins to make their tents (see Figure 4.22). They are semi-**nomadic** and move their animals in search of vegetation.

Inuit communities are found around the Arctic Circle, in Alaska, Canada, Greenland and parts of Russia. They fish and hunt for seals.

More recent settlers in cold deserts are more likely to rely on goods brought in from warmer parts of the country. For example, people in Oymyakon, in northeastern Russia, eat food brought in from further south and west where conditions are warmer and wetter and crops are grown and animals raised.

## Transport in cold deserts

Transporting resources into cold deserts is not easy. Ice and snow on roads can make driving dangerous. It can also be difficult to maintain roads built on permafrost. The thawing of the top layer of soil in the summer causes the ground level to change and the road to crack.

It is also difficult to bring goods in by sea as, during winter, it is so cold that the sea freezes. This means that boats cannot get into the ports.

People have to adapt by storing resources when they can get them, as they know they might be cut off from the outside world for months at a time.

▲ Figure 4.22 The Sami people rely on their herds of reindeer, including using the skins to make their tents

## 4 How does life adapt to its environment?

## Houses in cold deserts

Stone is hard to get in many cold desert areas, as rock is buried below frozen ground. Most modern homes are built with wood from nearby **boreal forests**. These homes are very well insulated to keep warmth inside.

Houses need to be built with permafrost-resistant foundations. In Oymyakon, many homes are built on stilts to prevent them from being damaged by melting permafrost. Here, water cannot be piped into homes as the pipes would freeze and burst. People collect and melt ice in the winter and collect water in the summer.

▲ Figure 4.23 Transporting goods by sea is difficult in winter.

### Key terms

**Boreal forests**: Conifer forests found in cold climates.

**Indigenous people**: Distinct groups descended from the original inhabitants of a place. They maintain unique languages, traditions and strong ties to ancestral lands.

**Nomadic**: People who move from place to place.

### Activities

1. Explain why it is difficult to get food in cold deserts.
2. Describe how houses are built to withstand the conditions of cold deserts.
3. 'It is harder to live in cold deserts than hot deserts.' To what extent do you agree with this statement?

## 4.7 What are the opportunities for people in cold deserts?

As well as adapting to survive in cold deserts, humans also find ways of creating opportunities in these extreme environments. But, as with hot deserts, the opportunities come at a cost.

## Mining for minerals

Some areas in the Arctic Circle have large deposits of valuable minerals, such as copper, nickel and gold. Many of these are in **inaccessible** locations due to their distance from population centres and because they are buried below the frozen **tundra**. However, improvements in technology and rising prices make accessing these minerals more cost effective.

## Oil and gas

As with minerals, previously inaccessible deposits of oil and gas are now being exploited. Many of these are in the Arctic Ocean and in areas that had been wilderness areas. It is difficult to transport oil from its source to where it is needed. The seas are often frozen so it cannot be taken by oil tanker, and pipes in the ground would freeze.

▲ Figure 4.24 An oil refinery on Alaska's north coast.

▼ Figure 4.25 An oil pipeline cuts through Alaska from north to south.

# 4 How does life adapt to its environment?

## Seed banks

The Global Seed Vault is on the Arctic island of Svalbard. Here, the seeds of over a million species of plant are stored deep below ground. If a disaster were to occur, these seeds could then be used to replace any plants that were made **extinct** elsewhere. Svalbard is an ideal location for a seed vault, as the low temperature and low level of moisture keep the seeds dormant.

## Conflict in cold deserts

As with hot deserts, there can be a temptation to view cold desert areas as uninhabitable wildernesses whose resources can be exploited by those who have the technology to overcome the challenges.

However, indigenous people have lived in these areas for thousands of years. Exploiting resources here puts their way of life at risk. It can reduce the land available for herding their reindeer, or can damage ecosystems, meaning there are fewer animals for them to hunt.

▲ Figure 4.26 The entrance to Svalbard's seed vault.

### Key terms

**Extinct**: A species that no longer exists.

**Inaccessible**: Difficult or impossible to reach and/or use.

**Tundra**: A cold region where trees do not grow.

### Activities

1. Explain why minerals and fossil fuel deposits in the Arctic had often not been exploited before.
2. Study Figure 4.25. Explain why an above-ground pipeline is needed to transport oil in this region.
3. Explain why cold deserts make a good location for a seed vault.
4. Explain why exploiting resources causes conflict in both hot and cold deserts.

# 4.8 What does the future hold for people living in extreme environments?

This chapter has explored how people adapt to life in the extreme environments of hot and cold deserts. However, environments are not fixed. They change. These changes mean that people have to continue to adapt to overcome new challenges.

## Climate change

Earth's climate is changing because of global warming. Many desert areas will become hotter and drier. This could make life even more difficult there. People are having to adapt by finding new water sources, such as making fresh water from seawater, and relying more on air conditioning to keep buildings cool. However, both solutions are expensive and need a lot of energy.

Unusually, the Thar Desert appears to be getting an increase in precipitation and there is a rise in the amount of vegetation growing there. While this is a positive thing for most people, most of the time, the heavy rainfall has caused sudden flash floods. It also means the habitat has changed for the plants and animals that have adapted to dry conditions. They may become extinct.

Temperatures are rising in the Arctic faster than they are elsewhere. This does bring some opportunities, as more land can now be **cultivated**

▲ Figure 4.27 Flash floods are becoming more common in the Thar Desert.

to grow crops. However, melting permafrost is damaging structures built on them (as they sink into the newly soft ground). There has also been an increase in forest fires affecting the region.

## Conflict over resources

As the world's population grows, demand for resources grows. This is especially a problem in areas where resources are already scarce.

▼ Figure 4.28 A map showing predictions for how affected regions of the world will be by temperature changes.

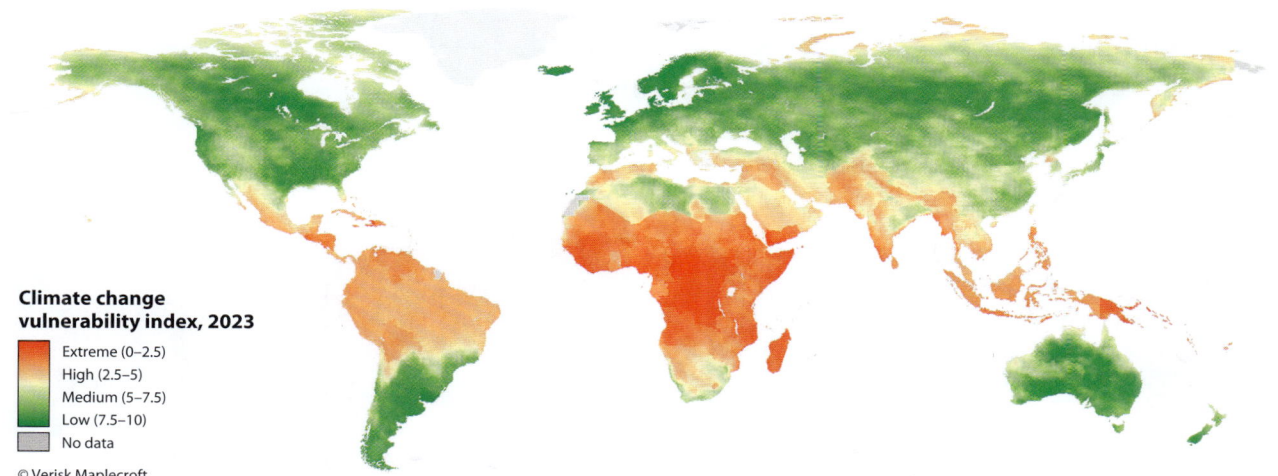

**Climate change vulnerability index, 2023**
- Extreme (0–2.5)
- High (2.5–5)
- Medium (5–7.5)
- Low (7.5–10)
- No data

© Verisk Maplecroft

## 4 How does life adapt to its environment?

For example, in hot deserts, one country might seek to take more water from a river to meet the needs of its population. This can cause conflict with other countries that share this river.

The building of the Grand Ethiopian Renaissance Dam on the Blue Nile will provide Ethiopia with hydroelectric power and a more reliable source of water. However, Egypt and Sudan are concerned that this will mean that less water will flow down the river into their countries. This could lead to conflict between these countries.

In the cold deserts of the Arctic, there is the potential for increased conflict over fossil fuel reserves. Thawing land and melting sea ice are making these reserves more available. This can cause conflict between those who want to exploit the reserves and the indigenous people who live within these countries. It can also cause conflict between countries that might both claim **sovereignty** over areas of the sea that contain these resources.

▲ Figure 4.29 Building dams on rivers has the potential to cause conflict.

### Key terms

**Cultivated**: Grown (plants), usually for commercial purposes.

**Sovereignty**: Power or authority over an area.

### Activities

1. Study Figure 4.28. Describe the trend in global temperature changes.
2. Create a table to show the economic, social and environmental advantages and disadvantages of the changes to hot and cold desert regions as a result of climate change.

# 4 End-of-chapter tasks

## Reflection

How does life adapt to its environment? You might like to consider the following points:
- How do plants and animals adapt?
- How are human adaptations different from the way plants and animals adapt?
- What challenges do humans create in their environments?
- Why might it become harder to adapt to extreme environments?

## Revision tasks

1 Create a spider diagram for hot deserts. Use the following stems:
   a Climate
   b Vegetation
   c Animals
   d Landscape
   e Challenges
   f Opportunities
2 Create a similar spider diagram for cold deserts.
3 Create a table showing the similarities and differences between hot and cold deserts. Use the same headings as your spider diagram for comparison.

## End-of-chapter review A

1 Study the climate graph (Figure 4.30) for China's Gobi Desert. **Describe** the climate. (3 marks)

2 Figure 4.31 shows the location of Greenland. **Describe** the location of Greenland. (2 marks)

3 **Explain** why Greenland has a cold desert climate. (4 marks)

4 Figure 4.32 shows a polar bear. This creature is native to Greenland. **Explain** how the polar bear has adapted to the cold desert climate. (4 marks)

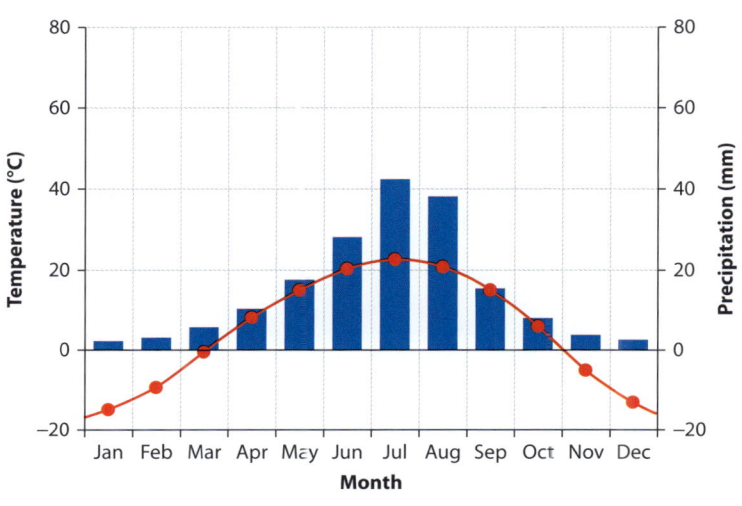

▲ Figure 4.30 Climate graph for the Gobi Desert, China.

## 4 How does life adapt to its environment?

▲ Figure 4.31 The location of Greenland.

## 4 How does life adapt to its environment?

▲ Figure 4.32 A polar bear.

▲ Figure 4.33 Taos Pueblo, New Mexico.

5 Figure 4.33 shows a house in New Mexico, USA. **Explain** how the house helps to overcome the challenges of living in a hot desert. (4 marks)

6 **To what extent** is climate change a threat to people who live in hot and cold deserts? (8 marks)

## End-of-chapter review B

Write a report comparing your local environment, and its impact on people, with either a hot or a cold desert. Your report should have the following sections.

- What is your climate like and how does it have an impact on the landscape? How is this different from either a hot or cold desert?
- How do plants and animals adapt to your local environment? Why do plants and animals in hot or cold deserts adapt differently?
- How does your local climate affect people? What are the advantages and disadvantages?
- How will climate change affect your local environment and the people who live there?
- Overall, does your local environment present more or fewer challenges and opportunities than a hot or cold desert environment?

# 4 How does life adapt to its environment?

## End-of-chapter review support

### End-of-chapter review A

Look at the number of marks available. Where the question is to 'describe', make as many points as there are marks available. Where the question asks you to 'explain', make two points and explain each one. The final question will be marked according to the overall quality of your response.

1. Describe how temperature and precipitation changes over the year and include the data.

2. Give two pieces of information that will tell someone where Greenland is located.

3. State one factor that affects the temperature of Greenland and explain how this affects the temperature. Do the same for precipitation.

4. State two adaptations that the polar bear has to the climate and explain how this helps overcome the challenges of living in cold deserts.

5. Give two adaptations that people have made to their houses in New Mexico and explain how this helps to overcome the challenges of living in hot deserts.

6. A good answer here will:
   - include both cold and hot deserts
   - explain how some people might benefit from a changing climate as well as those who will be threatened by it
   - include specific examples of activities that might be affected by climate change
   - reach a conclusion.

### End-of-chapter review B

A good report will have the following features:

- There is a focus on direct *comparison* between the local environment and one type of desert.
- There are specific details about the local environment, such as the climate or the plants and animals found there.
- The report justifies its conclusions about the potential future impacts of climate change. It draws on what was learned from Chapter 1.
- There is a good use of the key geographical terms from this chapter.

# 5 What can be done to ensure everyone has enough food?

## Chapter overview

### Why are you studying this?
Everyone needs to eat, but the ability to obtain enough healthy food varies across the world. In this chapter you will explore how and why food is not equally available to all and explore the idea of food security. Food production relies on fertile soil, but climate change and poor decisions by people are threatening its future productivity.

### Skills
In this chapter, you will learn about:
- using online data and mapping to explore patterns
- constructing line graphs
- how to interpret photographs as a form of geographic data.

### Learning outcomes
By the end of this chapter, you will understand:
- the global food supply system (GFSS) and why its resilience matters
- the significance of soil as a global resource
- the term 'food security', and why it varies around the world
- how climate change threatens future food production.

## What are the connections?
Future food production will be affected by climate change, which you explored in Chapters 1 and 2. Food production varies between climate zones, which you explored in Chapter 4, and also results in the loss of some habitats, such as tropical rainforest in locations such as Indonesia. In this chapter you will explore the benefits of living near volcanoes. You will learn more about volcanic eruptions in *Discover Geography 8*, Chapter 1.

## Where are you going?
Although the focus of this chapter is global, you will visit countries that have different levels of food security (their ability to feed themselves without relying on imports). For example, China is self-sufficient in some foods and exports food to other countries. The movement of food around the world will become increasingly important in the future. You will explore the importance of the global food supply system (GFSS) to New Zealand.

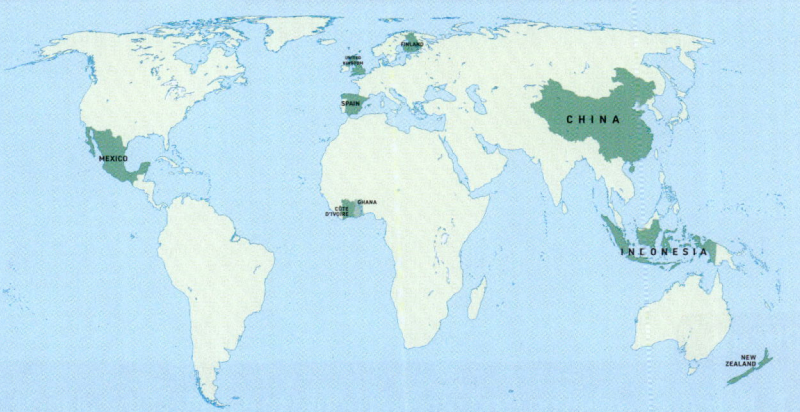

▲ *Figure 5.1 World map showing the locations of China, Finland, Indonesia, Spain, UK, New Zealand, Mexico, Côte d'Ivoire, Ghana.*

## 5 What can be done to ensure everyone has enough food?

### Is there enough food to feed everyone in the world?
As the world's population continues to grow, there is a need to produce more food.

- As food is not always produced where most people live, it is transported long distances, which has an environmental impact.
- While most people in high-income countries (HICs) have food all year round, lower-income countries (LICs) have more subsistence farmers, who depend on successful harvests for their food.
- Even in HICs, some people need support to obtain food, as prices vary more than they did in the past.
- There is inequality in the amount and types of food eaten in different countries. Overconsumption and waste help drive inequality in food security.
- Food production depends on a healthy soil and appropriate climatic conditions through the growing season. These are both becoming less reliable.

▲ Figure 5.2 Food waste can be turned into biofuels if collected effectively.

▲ Figure 5.3 Food often has to travel many miles from where it is produced to where it is consumed.

### Discuss

1 How does what you (and others) choose to eat affect the planet?
2 What processes and people are involved in supplying your meals? How sustainable are these in the long term?
3 Around one billion meals worth of food is wasted every day according to the United Nations. Where is food wasted in the global food supply system? How can we reduce this?

## 5.1 Is global food production keeping up with population growth?

As the world's population continues to grow, it is possible we will reach a point where there will not be enough food to feed everyone. In this lesson, you will explore how many people there are, and how much food must be produced to feed them all adequately.

### How rapidly is the world's population growing?

Every hour, 15 000 people are born. The world's population has grown very quickly from around 1 billion in 1800 to over 8 billion in 2025. Figure 5.4 shows the speed of recent growth. This creates pressure on governments to supply enough food for their population. Global food production must increase to keep pace with population growth.

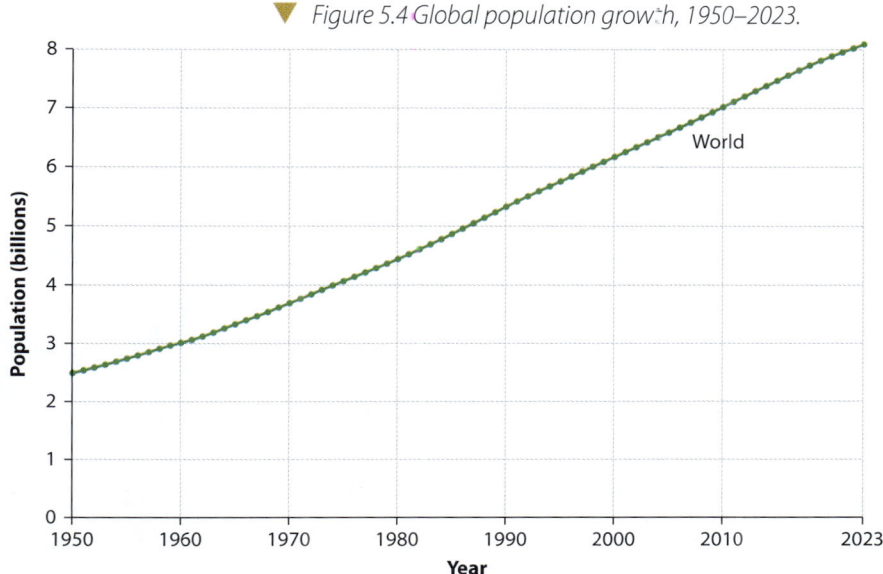

Figure 5.4 Global population growth, 1950–2023.

### How does food production vary?

Food production is unevenly distributed. Some countries can produce more than others. Countries grow food on their own farmland but also **import** food *from* other countries and **export** food *to* other countries. No country is **self-sufficient** in all the food it needs.

China produces large amounts of food as it has a large land area and varied climate. Other parts of the world produce far less food (see Figure 5.5), including Africa, the Middle East, Scandinavia and South America (outside of Brazil). The economy

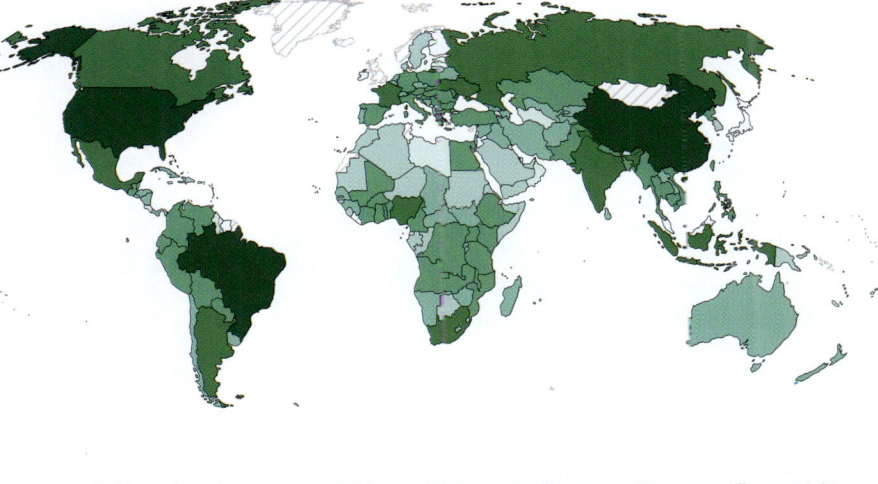

Figure 5.5 The total value of all the agricultural products, whether crops or animals, 2023. Measured in trillion dollars.

# 5 What can be done to ensure everyone has enough food?

of some countries relies heavily on food exports. (For example, the Solomon Islands are dependent on fish exports.)

## How has global food production been increased?

Since the 1950s, several agricultural developments have made land more productive. These include:

- new crop varieties which resist disease
- improved machinery and technologies to make farming more efficient
- more effective irrigation methods
- an increase in farmland by clearing other vegetation
- the development of new chemical fertilisers and pesticides.

## How will global food production change?

Food production in many parts of the world faces challenges in the next few decades. These include:

- Declining global soil fertility, affecting crop yields.
- Decreasing global soil moisture levels. Droughts are becoming more common. Farmers in some South America and Asian countries rely on rapidly melting glaciers for water.
- Rising global temperatures affecting crop yields.
- Conflict producing **food insecurity** by displacing farmers and making farmland unusable.
- Pressure on the global supply chain, which transports food around the world.

▲ Figure 5.6 Soil moisture levels are declining globally, reducing yields of vital cereal crops.

### Key terms

**Export**: Selling food to other countries.

**Food insecurity**: When people do not have regular access to enough good food.

**Import**: Bringing food into a country.

**Self-sufficient**: When a country can produce all the food it needs, without relying on other countries.

### Activities

1. **a** Look at Figure 5.4. In what years did the world's population reach 4, 6 and 8 billion?
   **b** At the current rate of growth, when is it likely to reach 10 billion?
2. What are some of the negative environmental impacts of food production?
3. How has food production been increased in recent decades?
4. Identify and explain **four** challenges that farmers will face in the next few decades, which may affect food production.

## 5.2 What is food security and why does it vary?

**Food security** is an indicator of whether a country is producing enough food to feed its population. It also shows how good a country's trading relationships are with other countries. All countries are **interdependent** and need food from other countries.

### What do we mean by food security?

The definition of food security was developed for the **United Nations** in 1996 (see Figure 5.7).

▼ Figure 5.7 The United Nations' definition of food security.

Food security exists when all people, at all times, have physical and economic access to sufficient, safe and nutritious food that meets their dietary needs and food preferences for an active and healthy life.

(World Food Summit, 1996)

The provision of food is not enough to ensure food security if it is not affordable, nutritious or physically accessible to all. This can be a problem in LICs, HICs and newly emerging economies (NEEs). Some communities in HICs may not have the opportunity to buy healthy food, or be able to afford it. There will always be a level of insecurity for some people.

### How does food security vary globally?

A Global Food Security Index (GFSI) has been developed by Economist Impact. This uses four factors to calculate scores between 0 and 100 for each country:

- food affordability (including people's ability to cope with price rises, and support available for those struggling to afford food)
- availability (agricultural production, risks of supply disruption and research to improve production)
- quality and safety (including the nutritional quality of the available food)
- sustainability (which includes how likely a country is to be affected by hazards, including climate change, which might affect production).

The best and weakest performing countries in the most recent index are shown in Table 5.1.

Syria and Yemen have both been affected by years of conflict, which degrades soil and disrupts farming.

| Best performers | Food security score |
|---|---|
| Finland | 83.7 |
| Ireland | 81.7 |
| Norway | 80.5 |
| France | 80.2 |
| Netherlands | 80.1 |

| Weakest performers | Food security score |
|---|---|
| Syria | 36.3 |
| Haiti | 38.5 |
| Yemen | 40.1 |
| Sierra Leone | 40.5 |
| Madagascar | 40.6 |

▲ Table 5.1 Countries with the highest and lowest Global Food Security Index scores in 2022.

# 5 What can be done to ensure everyone has enough food?

## Why does food security vary?

Many African countries, along with Venezuela, Syria, Yemen and Haiti, find it more difficult to source or grow enough food for their growing populations, sometimes due to conflict, or governance decisions. The USA, Western Europe, Japan and other HICs enjoy higher food security levels, and are more resilient to shocks caused by disasters. Figure 5.8 shows countries where the World Food Programme is working to improve food security.

Food insecurity arises from several factors, which are found to some extent in every country:

- Using farming methods which are not sustainable, such as reliance on chemical fertilisers to improve crop yields, which damages soil structure.
- Lack of government investment in, and support for, farming, which means farmers are not confident they will be paid appropriately.
- Farmland being replaced by land for other uses such as biofuels, solar farms and housing.
- Dependence on food imports, so countries are affected by price rises or changing relationships with trading partners.
- Climate change.
- Disruption to farming caused by conflict: for example, if land is mined.

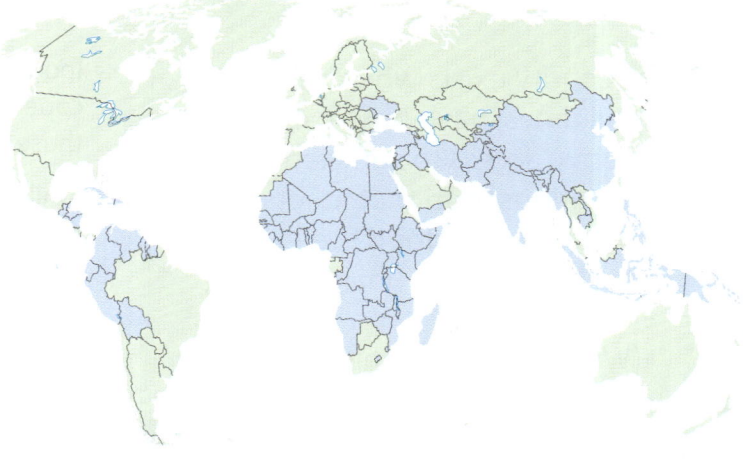

▼ Figure 5.8 A map showing countries, shaded blue, where the World Food Programme works to improve food security.

### Key terms

**Food security**: When people have regular access to enough good food.

**Interdependent**: When countries depend on each other.

**United Nations**: An international organisation founded in 1945 to promote peace, security and cooperation among 193 member countries.

### Activities

1. Look again at the definition of food security in Figure 5.7. Why do you think it is suggested that food security is 'almost impossible to fully achieve'?
2. Why you think Finland has such high levels of food security?
3. Figure 5.8 shows countries which the World Food Programme (WFP) is supporting. Which parts of the world do they work in?
4. Using the WFP website, identify the events, which could have been a hazard or other event, which led to the need for their support.

# 5.3 Why is soil so important?

A vital factor influencing food security is soil quality. The world's food relies on a couple of feet of soil, which covers 25 per cent of the surface of the Earth.

## Why is soil so important?

You may think of soil as unimportant, as it's just dirt or mud. However, the global population relies on food harvested from the 10 per cent of the Earth's land area where the soil is suitable for farming. This provides 95 per cent of the food people eat. Crops rely on soil for support, water and nutrients. Soil is home to more than half of all species, making it the largest habitat on the Earth. It is also a carbon store, particularly when in the form of a peat soil. It is possible to grow certain foods in nutrient-rich liquids – particularly salads and herbs – but this only occurs on a very small scale and requires a lot of specialist equipment.

▲ Figure 5.9 Crops such as maize require fertile soil to grow successfully.

## How are soils made?

**Soils** are made of four components occurring in different proportions depending on soil type:

- Weathered rock – produced by centuries of physical, biological and chemical weathering of local rock. It provides minerals needed by growing plants.
- Organic material from plants and animals, including the micro-organisms, fungi, bacteria and earthworms that live in the soil. It provides nutrients to growing plants.
- Water – the amount at different depths, and its ability to move through the soil vary.
- Air – without this, plants will not be able to survive. The pore spaces in soils allow water and nutrients to move to the roots of plants as they grow.

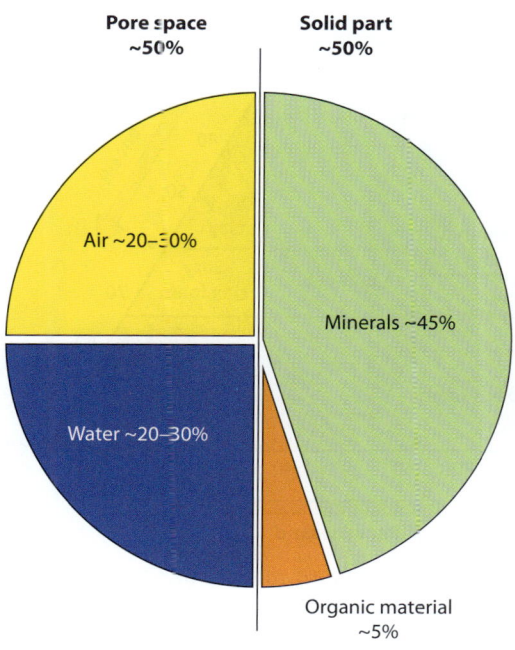

▲ Figure 5.10 The typical composition of soils used for agriculture/food production.

## 5 What can be done to ensure everyone has enough food?

Weathering of rocks creates a layer called regolith. This needs organic material to turn it into a soil that can grow food. Animal waste and animals' decomposing bodies provide organic matter. Earthworms turn the soil and aerate it. This all takes time – up to 400 years to produce 1 cm of soil. The same depth can be washed away in an hour by intense rainfall onto bare fields.

▲ Figure 5.11 Earthworms help to aerate the soil and mix organic matter into it.

### How many soil types are there?

Soils vary globally: the type, how deep it is and how fertile it is. Its fertility, in particular, affects food security. Soils can be classified by their texture (the relative amounts of sand, silt and clay), as shown in Figure 5.12. A loam soil, ideal for farming, will have a relatively even amount of each texture, so it is well drained and roots can grow through it easily.

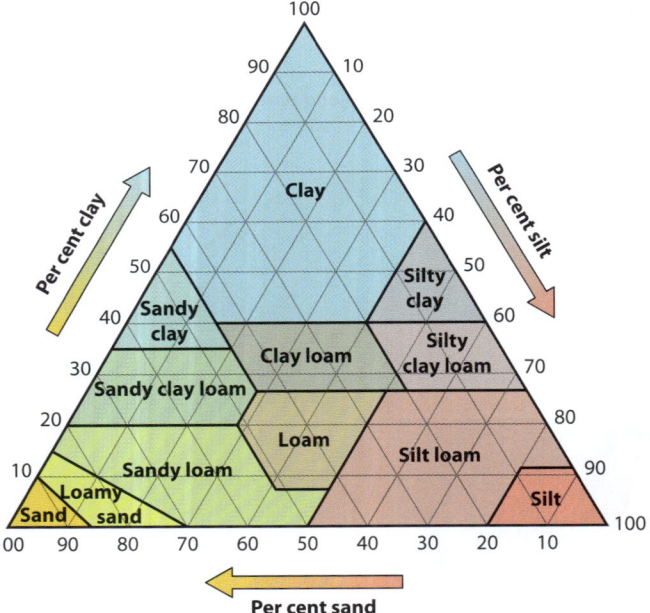

▲ Figure 5.12 The soil texture pyramid shows the relative amounts of sand, silt and clay, determining the soil type.

### Activities

1. Why is organic material important in the creation of fertile soils?
2. What are the four main components of a soil?
3. What does the soil texture pyramid show?
4. What is the typical structure of a loam soil like?

# 5.4 How are the world's soils changing?

Fertile soil is vital for agriculture. If topsoil is removed then food production is reduced. Topsoil is being lost due to three main processes: erosion, degradation and desertification.

## 1. Soil erosion

Soil is removed by water and wind. Fine soil is picked up by strong winds or soils can be broken up by heavy rain and washed down slopes. Farming methods which improve soil structure or protect the surface from heavy rain can slow erosion rates. These include avoiding ploughing down slopes, which would provide channels for rain to flow.

## 2. Soil degradation

Soil degradation is when the quality of the soil is lowered. Erosion is one example. It can also be caused by unsustainable farming, such as deforestation and overuse of fertilisers. In countries including Brazil and Indonesia, farmers and companies have cleared large areas of tropical rainforests for oil palm plantations or out of necessity. Machinery compresses soils, making them less likely to absorb rainfall.

## 3. Desertification

Forty per cent of the world's land is arid. Desertification turns productive land into unproductive desert. This results from poor soil management. Land most likely to become desertified is on the edge of deserts. Too many animals in one area leads to overgrazing, removing vegetation. Deforestation reduces rainfall, making areas hotter and drier. Trees may be removed for fuel, but planting trees can slow desertification

▲ Figure 5.13 Deforestation in Malaysia to make way for oil palm plantations.

Some local projects aim to improve water storage in soils. Semicircular pits called bunds are used in Kenya and Tanzania to store run-off after rainfall. It is vital to add organic matter to soil to help it hold on to soil moisture. Justdiggit funds this work.

## How does Indonesia benefit from volcanic activity?

Java and Sumatra are among the 17 000 islands that make up Indonesia. Volcanic eruptions, such as those of Mt Merapi and Mt Semeru (Figure 5.14), produce fine ash, which is deposited on their slopes. In the short term, this is a problem, burying crops and polluting water sources, but in the long term, soil fertility is increased.

## 5 What can be done to ensure everyone has enough food?

▲ Figure 5.14 Farms below Mt Semeru, Indonesia. Minerals in the ash mix with existing soils, which become very productive. Volcanic soils are found on just 1 per cent of the world's land, but feed over 10 per cent of the world's population, including areas such as Indonesia with very high population density.

### Activities

1 Explain the link between Indonesia's high population density and the fertility of the soil on its volcanic islands.

2 What are the main causes of desertification?

3 Suggest one strategy that allows farmers to reduce the likelihood of desertification.

4 🌐 If there is an opportunity to do this on the school site, supervised by teachers, dig a shallow soil pit to investigate the nature of the soil beneath your feet. You should find it has several layers (called horizons), with different thickness and colour, as well as texture. Investigate their organic content. Use a Geology map to find out what rocks lie below the soil, as they will affect its texture and quality.

### Key term

**Soil degradation**: A decline in soil quality, reducing its ability to support plants.

## 5.5 How does the global food supply system work?

The **global food supply system (GFSS)** is a complex web of activities involving the production, processing, transport and consumption of food. Food is produced in different parts of the world and transported by land, sea and air. Transporting food can lead to waste, excess packaging and carbon emissions, which contribute to climate change.

### Where does the food you eat come from?

You rely on the world to feed you. As particular climates and soils are needed to grow crops, every country has foods it cannot grow itself and has to import, but they will also export other foods. The trade in food may be unequal in terms of who benefits, which may unfairly affect some parts of the world. One way to think about the impact of food choices is to calculate the huge distances travelled by some foods. The concept of **food miles** was developed by Professor Tim Lang in the 1990s to quantify distances involved in the global food system, and economic and social impacts of food production. The implication is that eating locally is better for the planet, as it reduces the food miles.

### Why is global shipping so important?

The use of shipping containers speeded up the transfer of food between continents, reducing greenhouse gas emissions and transport costs. Refrigerated containers are used for fish and meat. Right now, 20 million containers are on the move. Trade deals are made within and between groups of countries called blocs. The largest of these is the Regional Comprehensive Economic Partnership (RCEP), which involves 15 countries including China, Japan, New Zealand and Singapore.

### What is the importance of the GFSS to Aotearoa New Zealand?

Much of Aotearoa New Zealand's farmland is pasture for cattle. It produces far more dairy products than its population could consume, so it exports them. It also exports kiwi fruit. They have a short growing season, so for several months, they are imported from Italy. Container ships arrive daily, bringing important foods from elsewhere:

- Rice arrives from Thailand and Australia.
- Sugar arrives from Australia and Thailand.
- Bananas arrive from Ecuador.
- Wheat arrives from Australia.

The GFSS allows this small remote country to trade important export crops with the world.

### What environmental impacts does the GFSS produce?

Food production creates 26 per cent of global greenhouse gas emissions, although only a small fraction comes from transportation. Food packaging waste is a problem. Although you might imagine tomatoes growing outside under the sun, they need help. The El Ejido region of Almeria in southern Spain has over 150 square miles covered in plastic greenhouses – visible from space – allowing multiple harvests (Figure 5.16).

▲ *Figure 5.15 Pastoral farming in Aotearoa New Zealand.*

## 5 What can be done to ensure everyone has enough food?

Figure 5.16 Greenhouses for salad production near El Eljido near Almeria in southern Spain.

- disruption due to COVID-19, resulting in lockdowns
- conflict in Ukraine increasing the price of key products it supplied, including sunflower oil and urea (used to produce fertilisers)
- fluctuating oil prices affecting costs of production and transportation
- climate change affecting harvests
- changes in political leadership meaning previous trade agreements being threatened, or new charges such as tariffs being added.

Three million tonnes of fruits and vegetables are grown here annually, including tomatoes, peppers and melons, to meet off-season demand across Europe. Water is pumped from underground to water crops. There are concerns about over-exploitation of migrant workers, over-use of chemicals and plastic sheeting being discarded carelessly, polluting marine ecosystems.

## What are the main threats to the smooth working of the global food system?

Feeding the world relies on the global food system operating smoothly. There have been 'shocks' to the system that have tested its resilience:

### Key terms

**Food miles**: The distance a food item is transported during the journey from producer to consumer.

**Global food supply system (GFSS)**: A complex web of activities involving the production, processing, transport and consumption of food within and between countries.

### Activities

1. Where does your family mostly buy food? What proportion do you think comes from the following sources:
   - supermarkets
   - smaller food retailers, including specialist shops such as butchers and bakers
   - markets
   - directly from farmers or producers?

2. Find at least **five** items which were **not** produced in your own country in your kitchen at home.
   a. Where were they produced?
   b. How do you think they made it to your home? How many food miles could have been involved?
   c. Mark the locations on a world map. Compare them with other students in your group.
   d. Which were the most common countries involved in producing the food you eat?

3. What are some of the 'shocks' that test the resilience of the global food system?

4. Why is the GFSS so important to remote countries like Aotearoa New Zealand?

## 5.6 How can a country improve its food security?

This lesson will explore how countries try to ensure food security or reduce insecurity. This involves reducing the impact of 'shocks' to the global food system, making countries more resilient.

### Why is food security so important?

You learned previously that there is currently enough food produced to feed everyone in the world, although it is not distributed fairly. Around a third of the food produced is wasted, mostly in HICs, and millions of people remain undernourished. Affordable food is not available for everyone.

Food insecurity can lead to a sense of desperation, which may affect society by adding to pressure on support services and governments, and reducing quality of life. Food insecurity leads to reduced **life expectancy**.

Food storage and transportation can cause waste. Not everyone has access to refrigeration. The equivalent of one billion meals a day are wasted or spoiled globally, many of them in HICs where less emphasis is placed on careful consumption of food.

### How can governments and organisations ensure food security?

Several methods are used by governments and other organisations to keep food affordable, including:

- Investing in research and innovation in food production, including automation, using drones and farming seafood rather than depleting wild fish stocks.
- Helping those who might struggle to access food at affordable prices, such as through **food banks**. These provide food parcels, containing basic meals for three days and other support services.
- Promoting healthy and sustainable eating to reduce over-consumption and poor diet choices in HICs.
- Looking for new trade deals which promise reliable supplies of food.

▲ Figure 5.17 Volunteer checking stock levels at a food bank in Yorkshire, UK.

Some charities produce free meals, using donated food as their ingredients. This may be food close to its sell-by date or be excess from farms. Organisations such as FoodCycle in the UK provide community meals, prepared by volunteers.

Governments in HICs should also support LICs in appropriate ways. Food insecurity is a cause of migration. It may cause people to move to HICs in the future. Food aid may be provided after disasters, along with investment in education for farmers. Not all of this aid might be effective.

# 5 What can be done to ensure everyone has enough food?

## What is Finland doing to ensure food security?

Some countries take extra steps to keep their food security high. In Lesson 5.2, you saw Finland's high food security score, although even here there is some food insecurity in low-income households. To maintain its score, Finland:

- prioritises local and sustainable sourcing of food, for example, in schools, which helps to educate young people about the need to reduce food waste
- provides financial incentives to farmers to move to organic production and invests in research and innovation in food production
- provides all Finnish children with free school meals
- invests heavily in free school meal programmes in other countries, including Central African Republic and Somalia
- has a National Emergency Supply Agency which has stockpiled eight months' supply of oats, wheat and barley in preparation for possible future shortages. Few countries have such stockpiles.

## Too Good to Go

*Too Good To Go* aims to tackle food waste. Founded in 2015 in Denmark, it operates in 19 countries across Europe and America. 100 million registered users and 175 000 active partner businesses are involved. Businesses share 'bags' of items which would otherwise be wasted. Users in the local area can buy them through a smartphone app and collect them later in the day.

### Key terms

**Food bank**: A place where those who are struggling to obtain enough food can go for support and food parcels.

**Life expectancy**: The average number of years a person born in a particular place will live.

▲ Figure 5.18 In Finland, the government provides all children with free school meals.

### Activities

1. How is a country's level of food security linked to its development?

2. The *Too Good To Go* app aims to tackle food waste. Suggest **five** other ways in which businesses in your own location could reduce the food waste they produce.

3. How is Finland preparing for the future and ensuring food security?

4. Produce a line graph to show the demand for food parcels provided by the Trussell Trust in the UK, based on the data in Table 5.2. Line graphs show the values of a single variable changing over time (in this case, the number of food parcels). Take care over the scale you use.

| Year | Food parcels (millions) |
|---|---|
| 2020 | 1.9 |
| 2021 | 2.6 |
| 2022 | 2.2 |
| 2023 | 3 |
| 2024 | 3.1 |
| 2025 | 2.9 |

▲ Table 5.2 Food parcels provided by the Trussell Trust.

# 5.7 Why does it matter what people choose to eat?

What you choose to eat matters. There is currently enough food to feed everyone, but some have access to more than others. Some eat unhealthily. Others have diets showing little variation. In conflict zones, people may rely on external aid. No one should go hungry, but decisions made by those in power have this consequence.

## Why are people's dietary choices important?

What you eat matters. Many people's diet in HICs is processed or **ultra-processed food (UPF)**. They are foods that have undergone multiple industrial processes and contain ingredients not commonly found in home cooking.

**Obesity** is a growing problem in some countries, putting pressure on health systems and reducing life expectancy. In the last few decades, more people have incomes which allow access to meat, dairy and processed foods. This increases demand.

Every shopping trip involves decisions, often linked to price. Some people make diet choices. Some decide to be **vegan** or vegetarian. However, choice is a luxury many people do not have. Changing diets have created increased demand for (and production of) fruits, vegetables, nuts and seeds.

▲ Figure 5.19 Avocados have a high water and carbon footprint when they are grown, added to by high food miles to most markets.

Any food has some impact on the environment when produced, but some have greater impact. Avocados grow in Central and South America. Global production has trebled in the last 20 years. Biodiverse forests are being cleared in areas such as Michoacán to increase production.

Avocado plantations rely heavily on fertilisers and chemicals to tackle pests. Even then, plants produce small yields increasing the carbon footprint per kg of fruit. They are a thirsty plant requiring 1000 litres per kg of fruit.

## Why might a vegetarian diet be better for the planet?

There is growing global demand for meat as a protein source. Meat production requires more land and water than any crop to feed the same number of people: 50–100 times as much land to produce the same amount of energy from beef as from plant-based alternatives. Land is also used to grow crops to feed to animals, rather than people. Livestock, particularly cows, are large emitters of methane (a greenhouse gas). Importing meat from overseas rather than eating local and seasonal food generates carbon emissions from the vehicles involved.

## Is eating insects a solution to food insecurity?

Over two billion people regularly eat insects as a source of protein. There are over 2200 edible species. Eating insects (which is called **entomophagy**) occurs in over 100 countries, particularly in Asia and Africa.

## 5 What can be done to ensure everyone has enough food?

Figure 5.20 Belalang goreng (fried grasshopper) is a meal served in some S.E. Asian countries.

Compared with farming beef or other meats, insects:

- are higher in protein than meat (between 40 and 75 per cent)
- are cold-blooded, so convert food to body mass more efficiently with less waste, and require far less food per kg of protein
- require much less water than cows (it takes over 15 000 litres of water to produce 1 kg of beef)
- can be ready to eat within days or weeks (a cow takes three years to reach the age where it can be eaten; they also multiply much faster)
- can be produced in urban environments on small scales, which means people can start a business at low cost.

If entomophagy is to become common, greater efforts are required to promote the benefits. Cricket flour can be used to make high-protein pasta which avoids people being presented with whole insects (see Figure 5.20). Insect farming is a low-cost way to increase food production.

## How can we reduce the environmental impact of dietary change?

Other important steps people could take to move towards more planet-friendly diets include:

- Reduce consumption of ultra-processed foods (UPFs), which use cheap ingredients, including palm oil. The production of palm oil has a dramatic impact on rainforests across Malaysia and Indonesia.
- Introduce educational programmes teaching young people the link between diet and health.
- More countries could copy France's 2016 Food Waste law, which prohibits supermarkets from throwing away food.
- Regulate fish farming to avoid environmental problems.

### Key terms

**Entomophagy**: Eating insects as part of the diet.

**Obesity**: Abnormal or excessive fat accumulation that causes a risk to a person's health.

**Ultra-processed foods (UPF)**: Food manufactured on an industrial basis, including chemical additives.

**Vegan**: Choosing to eat a plant-based diet, with no animal-related products, such as milk or eggs.

### Activities

1. Why has the demand for meat as a protein increased in recent decades?
2. Produce a comparison table which looks at the potential strengths and weaknesses of eating insect protein as an alternative to farming other animals.
3. What are UPFs, and what are the issues with having a diet where they make up a high proportion of what is eaten?

## 5.8 What impact might climate change have on future food production?

Currently enough calories of food are produced to feed everyone adequately. Climate change threatens to disrupt this and make farming impossible in some parts of the world. This could reduce food security, force a reliance on food aid or lead to migration or possible conflict. Reducing the increase of future temperatures is the best solution, but this would require global action, which seems unlikely.

### What are some of the impacts of climate change on farming?

Climate change is starting to change the crops that are grown in some countries as farmers realise that temperatures are too hot for what may have been planted before. Olives are now grown in Germany and rice has been grown in England. Some of the impacts of climate change on food production include:

- increases in temperatures, and prolonged periods of above-average temperatures, which slow the growth of crops
- changes in precipitation patterns, which may lead to crops receiving too little rainfall or too much (leading to diseases or farmers being unable to harvest crops)
- more extreme weather events, such as hailstorms (which can damage crops)
- unseasonal frosts, which can damage soft fruits in particular
- reductions in ground and surface water availability, which can lead to an increased need for irrigation, reducing groundwater levels.

▲ Figure 5.21 Flooded fields in Spain in 2024 following spring rainfall. Unpredictable rainfall is becoming more common.

## 5 What can be done to ensure everyone has enough food?

### How can climate change affect food production?

Climate change has a range of effects on food production:

- Crop yields are lowered, which may increase the price (affordability) of food and physical access to food.
- The quality of food can be reduced due to higher incidence of disease.
- Rising sea levels can lead to saltwater entering groundwater in coastal areas.
- More land has to be irrigated than before, which is causing water shortages in some locations.
- Crop diversity will be reduced as some crops will no longer be able to be produced in some locations.
- Some crops are particularly vulnerable to higher temperatures, including cocoa.

Cocoa only grows in a narrow band near the equator. In late 2023, intense rainfall led to an outbreak of black pod disease which damaged cocoa pods and reduced yields. Drought conditions affected West Africa in 2024 with record-breaking temperatures experienced in Côte d'Ivoire and Ghana, the two biggest producers of cocoa. The price of the main ingredient for chocolate rose 400 per cent in 2024, although farmers did not benefit from this. The price of chocolate has risen sharply, along with many other food crops.

Climate change may reduce the amount of food that is produced or increase food waste, for example, through damage to crops and livestock by the intensification of rainfall events.

◀ Figure 5.22 Chocolate prices rose by 400 per cent in 2024 after climate change affected harvests of cocoa pods in West Africa.

### Activities

1 How do the following aspects of a changing climate impact food production?
   a higher than average temperatures
   b prolonged dry periods or droughts
   c more extreme rainfall events, which may include thunderstorms or hailstorms

2 Why are chocolate prices likely to continue to rise in the coming years?

3 Research the possible impacts of climate change on agriculture in your location.

# 5 End-of-chapter tasks

## Reflection

Do you think it is likely that food production will continue to keep pace with global population growth, given the likely future impacts of climate change, and the unequal nature of food production?

## Revision tasks

1 Which parts of the world currently have the lowest levels of food security?
2 What makes the soil the most valuable resource that we have?
3 Why does it matter that global demand for meat is increasing rapidly?

## End-of-chapter-review A

1 **Suggest** three ways that food production has been increased in recent decades. (3 marks)
2 **Define** the term food security. (2 marks)
3 What are the four components that make up the soil? (4 marks)
4 What is entomophagy, and what are its benefits over other food sources? (4 marks)
5 **Outline** three challenges to future food production, and the strategies being used to reduce their impact. (6 marks)
6 Figure 5.16 in Lesson 5.5 shows the Almeria region of southern Spain. What are the social and environmental impacts of the food production methods shown here? (8 marks)

## End-of-chapter review B

Research one of the following options for improving future food security, or identify one of your own and produce a slide deck or poster.

1 Building shipping container farms such as those provided by Growcer (see their website) to produce food in a controlled environment.

2 Increasing rates of entomophagy in HICs as well as in LICs through promoting the benefits and marketing them effectively.
3 Vertical farming using hydroponics, which can be installed in buildings without requiring soil, and is a proven technology (Figure 5.23).
4 Large-scale fish farming inland, for example, tilapia production in Papua New Guinea.

▲ Figure 5.23 Vertical farming: growing food indoors without soil.

For each method, your slide deck or poster should outline:

a What are the benefits? How will it increase food production?
b What are the drawbacks? Does it have high start-up costs, for example?
c How suitable would it be for use across the planet, or would it be limited to particular locations?

## 5 What can be done to ensure everyone has enough food?

### End-of-chapter review support

#### End-of-chapter review A

Look at the number of marks available when considering your answer.

1. Suggest three methods which have been used to increase the productivity of the soil, or the people who farm the soil.
2. The UN definition of food security is quite complicated, but a simpler version would be acceptable.
3. There are four components in any soil, which will vary in amounts depending on soil type.
4. Start by defining the term and then think about three ways that the production of this type of food is more efficient than some alternatives.
5. Food production faces some future challenges. Identify three appropriate challenges, and for each one, match it with a strategy that is being used to reduce the impact.
6. Figure 5.16 shows the plastic greenhouses which are being used in southern Spain to produce crops for export. For each of the impacts, provide a negative and a positive example.

#### End-of-chapter review B

You will need to assess to what extent each of the ideas you explore is:

- practical – this must be something which is possible and not science-fiction (for example, moving everyone to another planet)
- scalable – while it may have been tried on a small scale already it needs to be suitable for a large enough scale to produce food for hundreds of millions of people
- affordable – how much does this cost compared with traditional farming methods. Is there a need for extra infrastructure, labour costs, technology, energy etc.?

# 6 What impacts will a changing climate have?

## Chapter overview

### Why are you studying this?

In Chapter 1, you discovered that the climate is changing and that recent change is a result of human rather than physical factors. In this chapter, you will explore how this change in the physical environment impacts people.

### Skills

In this chapter, you will learn about:

- how geographers classify different impacts
- how to interpret data located on world maps and shown in compound bar graphs.

### Learning outcomes

By the end of this chapter, you will understand:

- how geographers classify impacts
- the interconnected nature of planetary health
- some environmental, economic and social impacts of climate change
- the impacts that climate refugees face
- the impacts that climate change has had in Russia.

## What are the connections?

This chapter links back to Chapter 1, where you started to explore how different places were affected by climate change. It also links forward to *Discover Geography 9*, Chapter 2, where you will complete the circle and look at how people can respond to a changing climate and its impacts.

## Where are you going?

In Chapter 1, you looked at a changing climate from a general, global perspective, but also focused on Russia and the Middle East. In this chapter, you will focus on the impacts of a changing climate in Russia in particular.

▲ Figure 6.1 Map of the world showing the location of Russia.

# 6 What impacts will a changing climate have?

## Climate extremes

Extreme natural events seem to be increasing as a result of climate change. These range from flooding to wildfires and impact the people that live in the areas affected. However, the impacts of climate change can also be smaller and less dramatic, but still have a significant effect on people.

▲ Figure 6.2 Summer temperatures in Delhi, India can be very hot.

▲ Figure 6.3 Flooding in Florida, USA as a result of climate change.

▲ Figure 6.4 A wildfire in Siberian Russia, near Novosibirsk.

### Discuss

1. Have you noticed any changes to the climate in the area where you live?
2. Can you think how animals or plants could be affected by these changes?
3. How do you think climate change could affect your favourite outdoor activities?

## 6.1 How can we classify the impacts of climate change?

Before you start to explore some of the impacts of climate change, you need to understand how geographers think about impacts and how to classify them. This helps you to organise information and make comparisons between different places.

## Defining impacts

In geography, an impact is the effect an event has on a particular place or group of people. The impacts of a changing climate include the more extreme weather you learned about earlier, leading to flooding or wildfires, flowers blooming earlier in the season or having to wear different clothing when doing your favourite outdoor activity.

You will notice that these impacts are very different: some are large scale while others are smaller scale, some have devastating effects while others do not, some affect natural processes while others influence human activity. Because we live in a messy world and the list of impacts could be very long, geographers classify impacts to make sense of them and to make comparisons.

## Classifying impacts

There are several ways geographers classify impacts, starting with whether they are positive or negative. Unfortunately, when we are talking about the impacts of climate change, most of

▲ Figure 6.5 Flowers blooming earlier in the season does not seem to be a significant impact. However, it can disrupt food webs, increase frost risk and use up soil moisture early in the season.

# 6 What impacts will a changing climate have?

them are negative – they have a harmful consequence on people and the environment. This can feel quite depressing, but it is important to identify and understand negative impacts so that we can take steps to reduce these harms. It may also bring some positive impacts, although by identifying them we are not saying that climate change is a good thing.

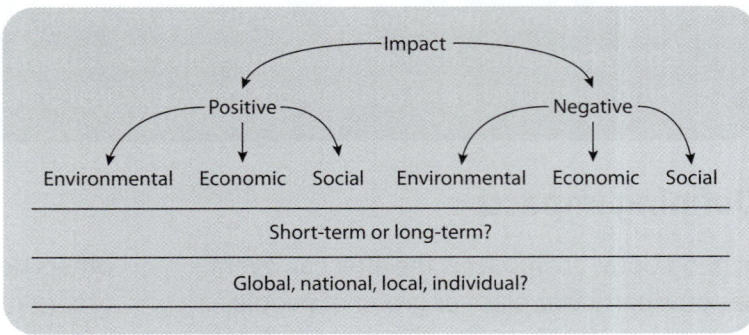

▲ Figure 6.6 Classifying geographical impacts.

Once geographers have decided whether an impact is positive or negative, they sort them into categories to say whether the impact is environmental, economic or social. Environmental impacts are the effects climate change has on the natural world, such as coral bleaching or sea-level rise leading to coastal flooding. Economic impacts are to do with money and jobs, so include the effects on tourism or agriculture. Social impacts are to do with people, so include the effects that climate change has on health. However, it is important to understand that impacts often fit into more than one category.

Geographers can classify impacts further, into short- or long-term impacts – consequences that happen quickly, or those that take longer to have an effect. In terms of climate change, even short-term impacts can take years to be noticed. This is why you may have found it difficult to answer the question about this at the start of the chapter.

You can also classify impacts by scale – whether they will have a global, national, local or individual effect. While climate change will affect everywhere to some extent, some areas and people living in them will be more vulnerable.

Once they have finished classifying impacts, geographers can **weight** them. This means thinking about which impacts will have more effect and giving them a higher score to show they are more significant.

### Activities

1. Why is it important for geographers to categorise impacts?

2. Write down some different impacts of climate change on small pieces of paper or sticky notes, one for each impact. Follow the classification diagram in Figure 6.6 to sort your impacts into different categories.

3. Write **three** sentences to summarise your conclusions. For example, are there more positive impacts or negative ones? Are the impacts mainly environmental, economic or social? Which is the most significant impact?

4. What might be a problem with drawing a conclusion in this way?

### Key term

**Weight**: How important something is in terms of its impact – some impacts are considered more significant and are given more 'weight'.

## 6.2 What is the health of the planet?

The impacts of climate change are interconnected. This means that one impact can have knock-on effects on others. One way of looking at this is by exploring planetary health.

### Feedback loops

In Chapter 1, you learned about feedback loops. These are processes where a change causes impacts that increase or reduce the original change. There are two types of feedback loop. Positive feedback loops make the initial effect stronger. For example, as the planet warms, ice melts, exposing darker surfaces that absorb more heat, which leads to even more warming and further melting. However, there are also negative feedback loops which reduce the effect of changes. For example, an increase in temperature might lead to more cloud cover, which reflects sunlight and can help cool the Earth.

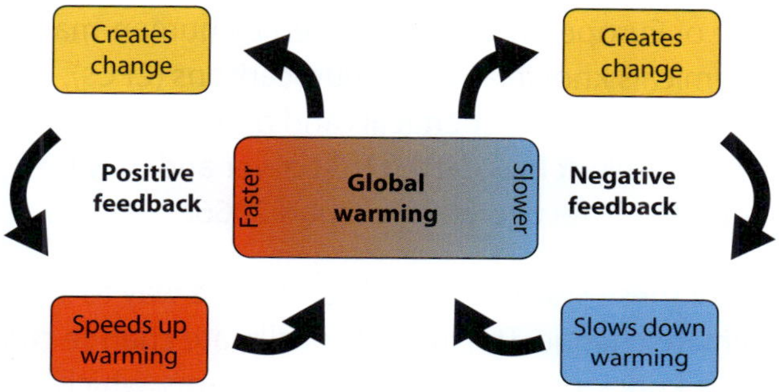

### Tipping points

When a positive feedback loop becomes strong enough, it can push a system past a **tipping point**. These are important **thresholds** within the Earth's climate system. Once they have been crossed, they can trigger large, rapid and often irreversible changes. These tipping points are dangerous because a relatively small change, such as a slight increase in temperature, can push a system past its threshold.

▲ Figure 6.7 Positive and negative feedback loops.

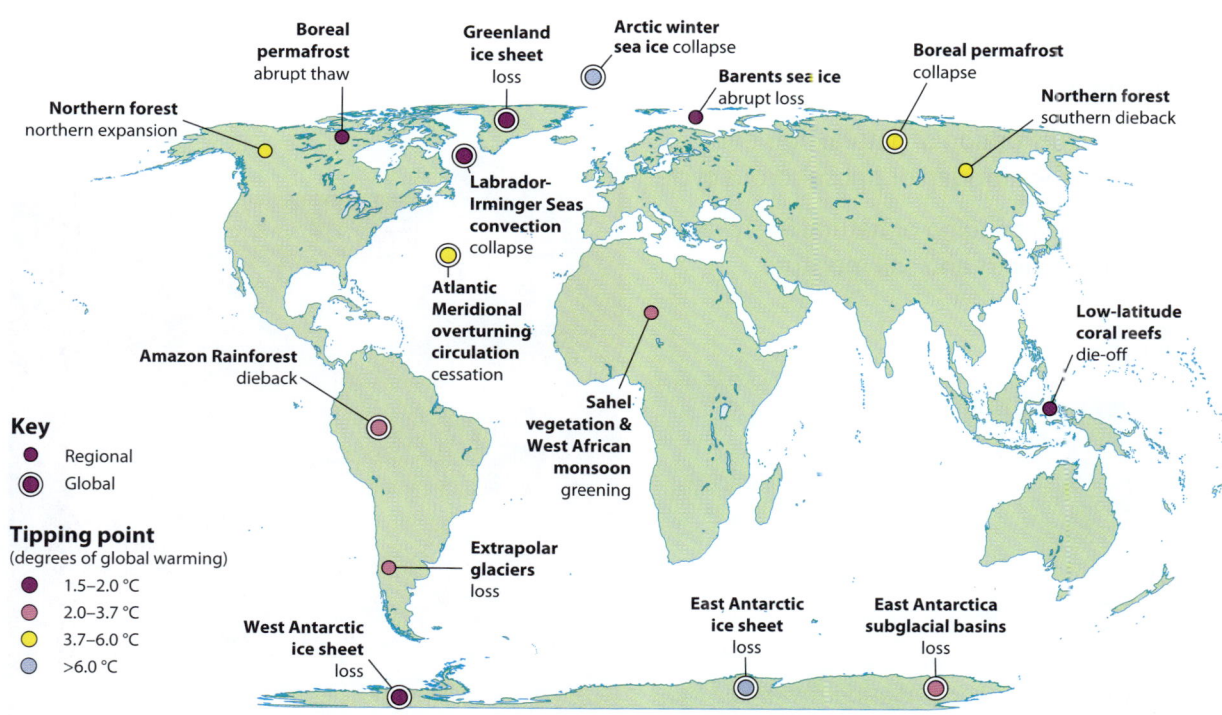

▲ Figure 6.8 Possible climate tipping points.

# 6 What impacts will a changing climate have?

Some examples of climate tipping points are shown in Figure 6.8. They include the melting of the Greenland and West Antarctic ice sheets, which could lead to significant sea-level rise, or the thawing of permafrost leading to the release of large amounts of the greenhouse gas methane.

## Planetary health check

A planetary health check looks at the overall health of the Earth and its systems. These include:

- climate change – the amount of greenhouse gases in the atmosphere
- pollution – the amount of pollutants in the atmosphere
- **ozone layer depletion** – the thinning of the ozone layer, which allows UV radiation to reach the Earth's surface
- aerosols – the amount of particles in the air, which can affect patterns of temperature and precipitation
- ocean pH – changes in ocean conditions, such as acidification, biodiversity and its capability to regulate climate
- nutrients – the disruption of natural nutrient cycles, such as the nitrogen or phosphorous cycle
- fresh water – the changing of natural freshwater cycles, including rivers and soil moisture
- land use – the transformation of natural landscapes through urbanisation or deforestation
- biosphere – the decline in diversity, extent and health of ecosystems.

A planetary health check report is created each year. In the 2024 report, three of the nine systems are operating safely, while the other six are not safe. However, it is possible to make unsafe systems safe again. For example, ozone layer depletion: until 2000, the ozone layer had a massive hole in it that was around seven times the size of Europe, which was caused by human-made chemicals known as chloroflurocarbons (CFCs). By banning these chemicals and monitoring the hole closely, it has started to recover and may be completely recovered by around 2066.

All of these systems are linked in some way to climate change. The impacts of climate change can have knock-on impacts in other systems, which can trigger feedback loops and eventually tipping points.

### Key terms

**Ozone layer depletion**: The gradual thinning of the ozone layer in the Earth's upper atmosphere caused by human-made chemicals called CFCs.

**Threshold**: Marks the boundary between one thing and another.

**Tipping point**: Where a threshold is crossed which can lead to large, rapid and irreversible changes.

### Activities

1. Look at Figure 6.8. Which of these tipping points is likely to happen first? How do you know?
2. Each of the categories in the planetary health check has a link to climate change. Draw a spider diagram with climate change in the centre and the categories around the outside. Join these to climate change with arrows and, along each arrow, write the link the category has to climate change.
3. Put 'Planetary health check' into a search engine and find the latest report. Carry out some research to see how planetary health has changed over time.

# 6 What impacts will a changing climate have?

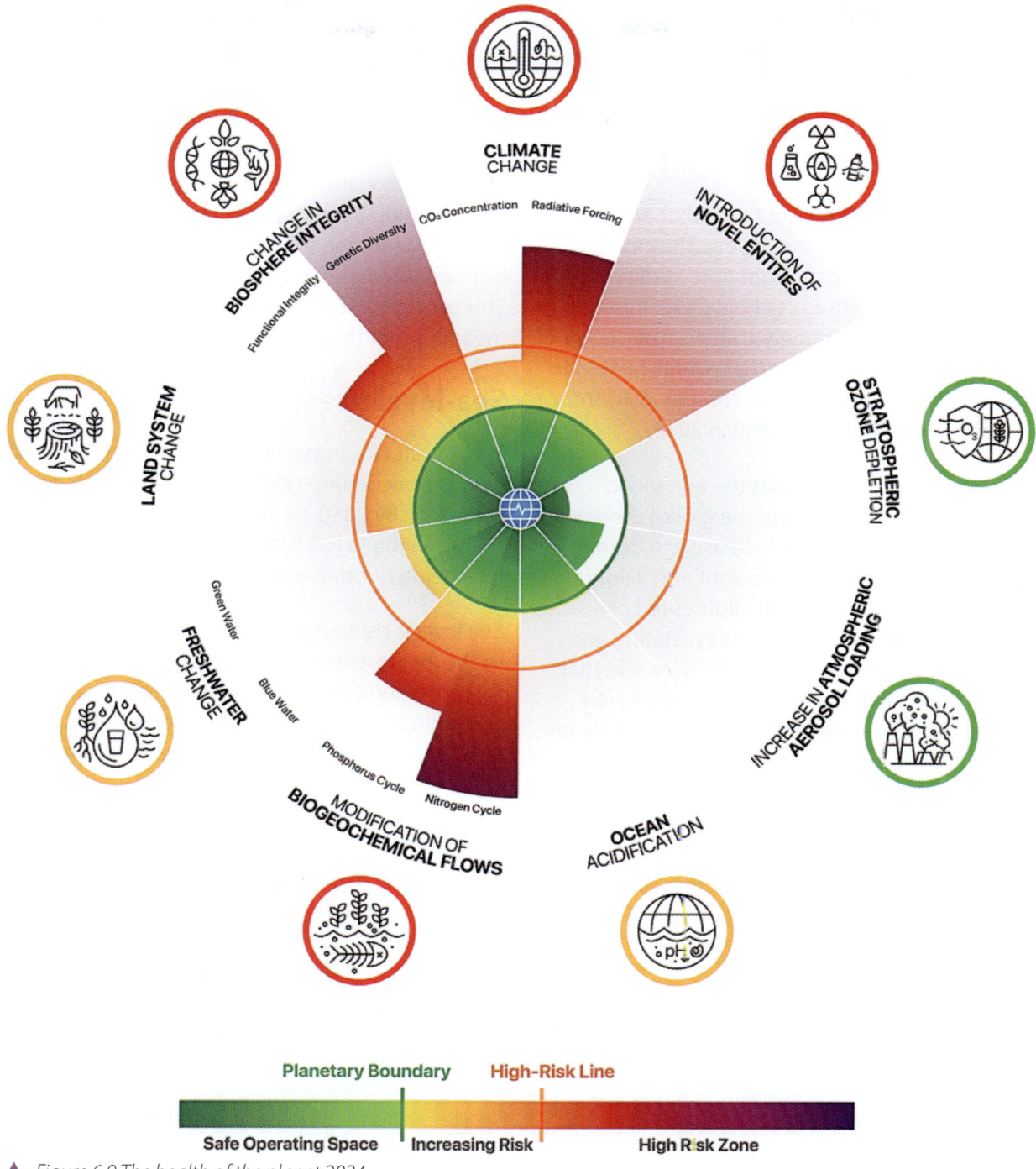

▲ Figure 6.9 The health of the planet 2024.

## 6.3 What are some environmental impacts of climate change?

This lesson explores some of the environmental impacts of climate change, including the increase in extreme weather events and sea-level rise.

### The increase in extreme weather events

Extreme weather events are those that are rare for a particular place and time of year. They include: heatwaves, leading to drought and wildfires; intense storms, which cause heavy precipitation and flooding; and extremely cold weather. Look at Figure 6.10, which shows that events related to climate change have increased dramatically from around 250 in 1980 to over 800 in 2019.

You learned in Chapter 1 that the enhanced greenhouse effect is causing the global average temperature to rise, so the increase in extreme temperatures, heatwaves, drought and wildfires is understandable. The 2024 wildfires in Los Angeles, USA were particularly devastating and destroyed 1716 houses. Scientists have said that the conditions that resulted in these fires were made about 35 per cent more likely due to climate change.

**Tropical storms** are also increasing as a result of climate change. This is because they get their energy from warm, wet air over the ocean (Figure 6.11). As global temperatures rise, more of the world's oceans reach or exceed 27 °C, which is the temperature needed to create a tropical storm. This provides more energy for the storms to form, meaning that they are larger and last for longer.

### Sea-level rise

Tropical storms impact people living on the coast, who are becoming more vulnerable due to rising sea levels. By 2050, there could be 300 million people living in low-lying coastal areas who could face being flooded every year.

Sea level is rising due to two processes linked to the increase in global average temperature. As Earth's temperature increases, land ice in Greenland, Antarctica and mountains melts at a faster rate. This flows into the oceans, adding to

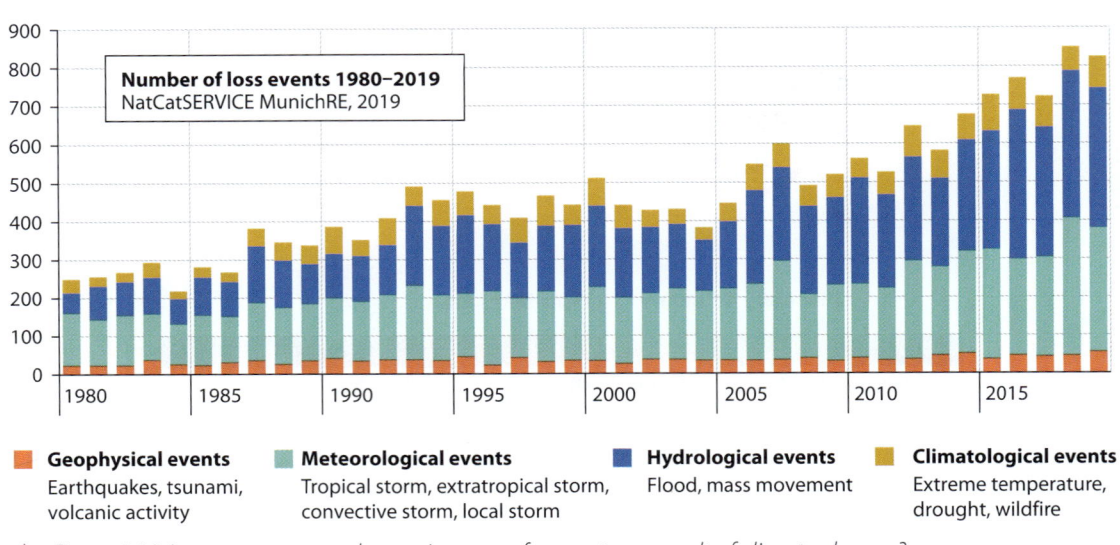

▲ Figure 6.10 Are extreme events becoming more frequent as a result of climate change?

## 6 What impacts will a changing climate have?

◀ Figure 6.11 Tropical storms are becoming larger and more intense as a result of climate change.

▼ Figure 6.12 The low-lying islands of Kiribati are vulnerable to sea-level rise.

the total volume of seawater and raising sea levels. At the same time, oceans absorb about 90 per cent of the heat trapped by greenhouse gases. As water warms, it expands and this causes seawater to take up more space, which causes sea levels to rise even further.

Over the past 30 years, sea levels have risen by 5–11 cm and are estimated to rise by a further 50 cm to 2 m by 2100. Kiribati's islands are extremely low lying, with most land less than two metres above sea level. This makes them at risk of flooding and erosion. Two islands have already disappeared, and regular storm surges affect inhabited areas, contaminating fresh water, damaging crops and flooding homes.

### Activities

1. Describe the pattern shown on the graph in Figure 6.10. Why are geophysical events fairly stable?

2. Use a search engine and search for 'Floodmap'. This will give you a map showing which parts of the world will be affected by different levels of sea-level rise. Adjust the water level to explore what happens. By how much does sea level need to rise for your country to be impacted?

3. Explain why an increase in extreme weather events and sea-level rise are environmental impacts of a changing climate.

### Key term

**Tropical storms**: Powerful storms in the tropics with heavy rain, strong winds and flooding.

113

## 6.4 More environmental impacts of climate change

This lesson explores some more of the environmental impacts of climate change, including coral bleaching and mangrove destruction.

### Mangroves

Mangroves are coastal forests found in tropical regions. If sea levels rise too quickly, mangroves find it difficult to adapt and this leads to a loss of habitat and threatens biodiversity.

The tropical storms you learned about earlier can damage mangrove forests. If they become more frequent, it is harder for the trees to recover. In the last 50 years, 35 per cent of mangroves have been destroyed and one in five are endangered. Mangroves act as natural barriers against storms and erosion. If they are lost, this increases the vulnerability of people living near the coast to extreme weather and rising seas. Around 120 million people living in countries such as Indonesia rely on mangroves for food and income. Local communities harvest fish, crabs and shrimps from mangrove swamps.

### Coral bleaching

Coral bleaching is a stress response in which corals lose their vibrant colours and turn white. A type of algae called zooxanthellae live on corals and provide their colour and most of their energy through **photosynthesis**. When water

▲ Figure 6.13 Mangrove forests are vulnerable to sea-level rise.

## 6 What impacts will a changing climate have?

▲ Figure 6.14 A healthy coral reef (left) and one that has been bleached (right).

temperatures rise beyond what corals can tolerate, they become stressed and expel the algae. Without these algae, corals become white or 'bleached' and are more susceptible to disease and death.

Even a small rise in sea temperature – often just 1 °C – can trigger bleaching. While temperature is the main factor, pollution and changes in ocean chemistry (called **ocean acidification**) can also lead to bleaching. The fourth global coral bleaching event, in 2024, is the most widespread and intense on record, impacting 84 per cent of the world's reefs.

### Key terms

**Ocean acidification:** The reduction in the pH of the ocean, caused by the absorption of carbon dioxide from the atmosphere due to human activities.

**Photosynthesis:** The process where green plants convert sunlight, carbon dioxide and water into glucose and oxygen, releasing energy essential for life.

### Activities

1. Explain the process of photosynthesis. Why is it an important process for mangroves and coral reefs to thrive?

2. Carry out some research into either mangroves or coral reefs. Create a poster to summarise what you find out. Try to include what the problem is, the causes of the problem, who and where will be affected, and the knock-on consequences of this.

3. Explain why mangrove destruction and coral bleaching are environmental impacts of a changing climate.

# 6.5 What are some economic impacts of climate change?

You are now going to explore some of the economic impacts of climate change. In particular, you are going to look at the impact on agriculture (which links to Chapter 5) and tourism.

## The impact on agriculture

If we do not do anything about climate change, global **GDP** could decrease by up to 10 per cent by 2100. Although most people would be affected, people in Africa and Asia would be particularly vulnerable. This is because one of the most significant economic impacts is on agriculture, which is the farming of crops and animals, often for food.

Rising temperatures, more frequent heatwaves, droughts and erratic rainfall patterns are leading to a decrease in crop yields of rice, wheat and maize. These are known as staple crops, meaning that they make up a large proportion of nutrients in a person's diet. This threatens food security as it means that costs are likely to be higher. About 26 per cent of the total working population work in agriculture, so this will also have an impact on their jobs. In some parts of Africa this figure is over 70 per cent, meaning that the impact will not have the same economic consequences everywhere.

However, the impacts of climate change on agriculture are not all negative. In some temperate regions, rising temperatures are extending the period in which the ground is free of frost. This leads to longer growing seasons, which means farmers can generally grow more crops in the year.

## The impact on tourism

Tourism supports more than 255 million jobs worldwide. However, climate change is affecting places that might attract tourists, such as low-lying tropical islands, coastal areas and coral reefs.

In mountainous regions, rising temperatures have led to snow melting, threatening ski resorts, particularly those in the Alps and in North America. The ski season is around 36 days shorter and 13 per cent of resorts are predicted to lose all of their natural snow by 2100.

These changes have meant that tourists are avoiding areas which are prone to extreme heat or environmental hazards.

▲ Figure 6.15 Rice farming in Indonesia.

## 6 What impacts will a changing climate have?

▼ Figure 6.16 Deogyusan ski resort in South Korea.

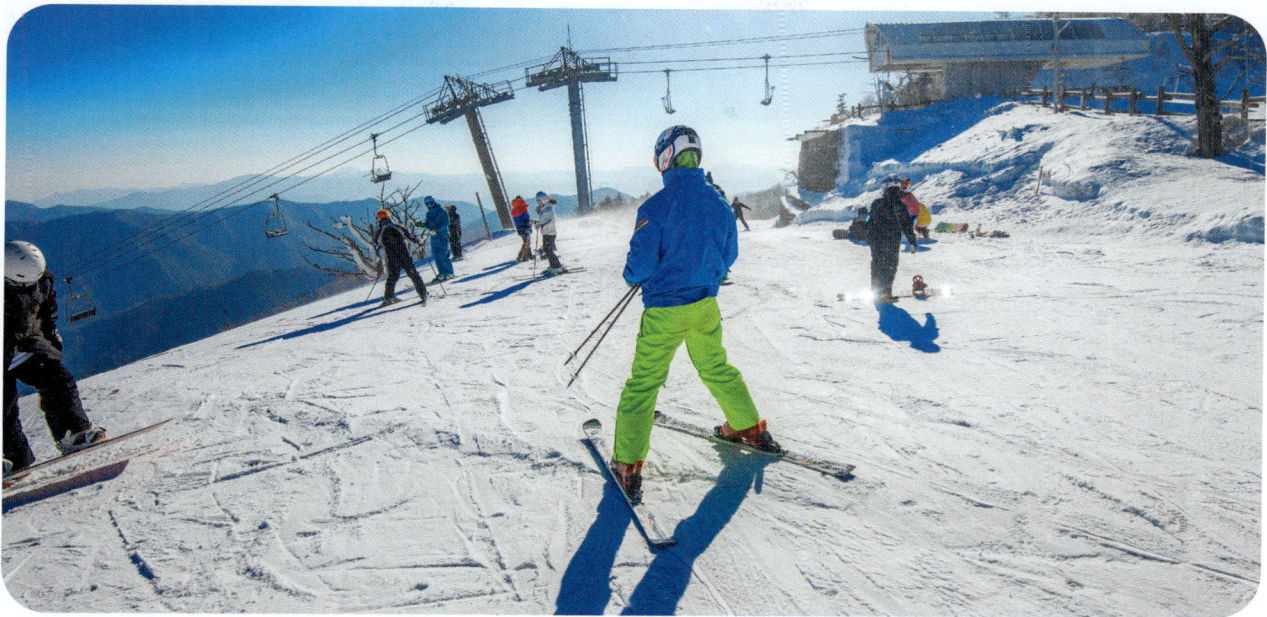

### Key term

**GDP:** Stands for Gross Domestic Product, which is the total monetary value of all goods and services produced within a country, usually in a year.

### Activities

1 Look at Figure 6.15. Rice is a staple crop in Indonesia. What does this mean?
2 If crop yields reduce as a result of climate change, what is likely to happen? Complete the 'chain of reasoning' diagram to show the knock-on effects. Make sure you use your knowledge from Chapter 5 too.

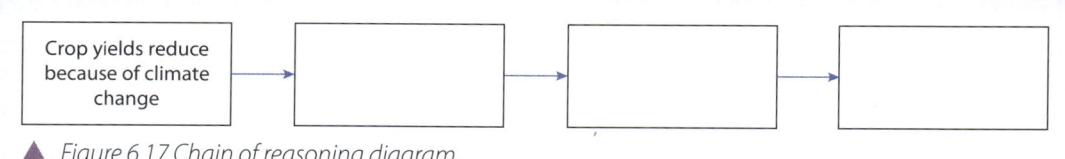

▲ Figure 6.17 Chain of reasoning diagram.

3 Imagine you were going on holiday to a ski resort such as the one shown in Figure 6.16. Write down a list of the different jobs that people would need to do to make sure you had a good holiday. Do not forget jobs such as pilot and cleaner!
4 If the ski resort you were going to was affected by climate change, what do you think the economic impacts of this would be?

## 6.6 What are some of the social impacts of climate change?

Having looked at environmental and economic impacts, you are now going to look at some social impacts of climate change.

### Health risks

Climate change is not good for our health. Between 2030 and 2050, it will cause approximately 250 000 additional deaths per year: that is, 14.5 million extra deaths. Mostly, this will be due to reduced food security and undernutrition, but heat stress and diarrhoea are likely to increase too. Vulnerable groups – such as the elderly and low-income populations – are likely to suffer the most.

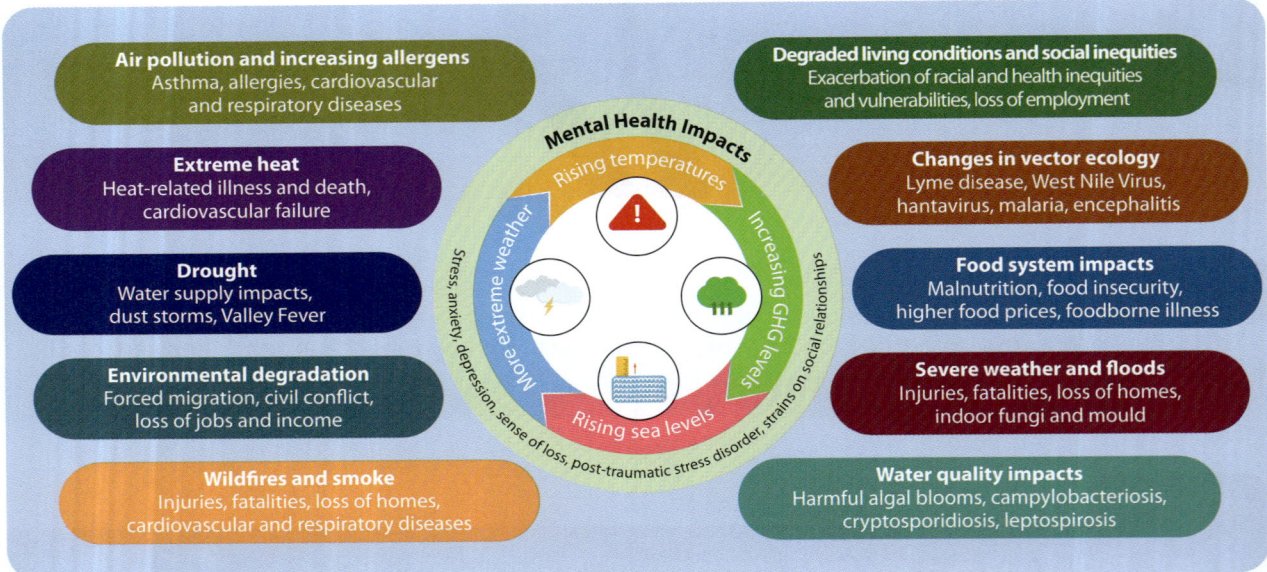

▲ Figure 6.18 Some of the impacts of climate change on human health.

Malaria is a disease which is likely to increase as a result of climate change. Between 2024 and 2050, climate change could lead to 123 million more malaria cases and 532 000 more deaths in Africa alone.

This is because warmer temperatures encourage the malaria-carrying mosquitoes to breed more quickly and this increases the risk and rate of transmission. Changes in rainfall patterns, including increased flooding and erratic rainy seasons, also create more **standing water**, which provides perfect breeding conditions for mosquitoes.

Climate change is having a growing impact on mental health. Experiencing disasters such as floods, wildfires, hurricanes and heatwaves can lead to trauma, depression and anxiety. For example, following the California Camp Fire in 2018, 67 per cent of people who were directly impacted reported trauma.

Even those not directly affected by climate-change-related disasters experience anxiety, grief and helplessness about the future. 84 per cent of young people globally are worried about climate change, with 59 per cent being extremely worried.

# 6 What impacts will a changing climate have?

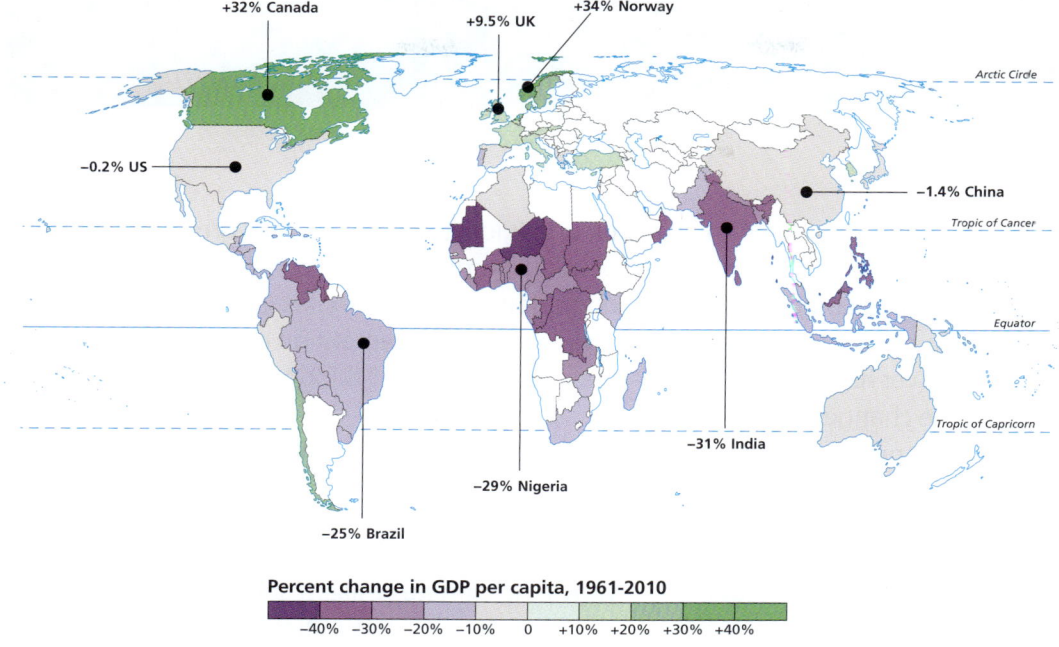

▲ Figure 6.19 The inequality of climate change.

This is unsurprising given that the majority of impacts you have learned about in this chapter have been negative ones. However, there is hope for the future in addressing these problems. You will find out more about this in *Discover Geography 9*, Chapter 2.

## Increased inequality

The word 'vulnerable' has been used a lot in this chapter. This is because the impacts of climate change tend to affect some people more than others. Under-resourced groups – such as low-income households, women and indigenous peoples – are more likely to be more exposed to climate hazards and have fewer resources to cope and recover. They are more vulnerable.

The result is that climate change makes **inequalities** within a country and between countries greater. Globally, those least responsible for climate change – mainly people in low- and middle-income countries – are the hardest hit, whereas wealthier countries, that have contributed most to emissions, are better able to adapt and recover (Figure 6.19).

### Activities

1 Look at Figure 6.18. For one of these categories of impact on health, write a list of those people who are likely to be vulnerable.

2 Carry out some research about one of the impacts of climate change on health. Use 5Ws (Who? What? Where? When? Why?) and an H (How?) to structure your research.

3 Look at Figure 6.19. Describe the pattern on the map. What does this tell us about the inequality of climate change?

### Key terms

**Inequalities**: Differences in access to resources, opportunities or rights among individuals or groups, often leading to social or economic disadvantage.

**Standing water**: Stagnant water that collects and provides breeding grounds for mosquitoes.

## 6.7 What are climate refugees?

The issue of climate refugees links some of the environmental, economic and social impacts that you have explored already in this chapter.

## Climate refugees

Climate refugees are people who are forced to leave their homes due to changes in their local environment caused by climate change. Since 2008, more than 376 million people have been displaced by disasters, and over half of these have been related to climate change. This figure is rising, with up to 1.2 billion people being displaced globally by 2050.

Despite the growing scale of the crisis, there is no agreed definition of what a 'climate refugee' is. This means that people who are displaced are not protected by the **Refugee Convention**, which only covers those fleeing persecution based on race, religion, nationality, social group or political opinion. Some people also feel that, because migration is such a complex issue, pinning the reasons for displacement on climate change alone may not be the right thing to do.

International organisations like the United Nations High Commissioner for Refugees (UNHCR) and **non-governmental organisations (NGOs)** such as the Red Cross, support displaced people by providing climate-resilient shelters and access to clean water. Communities are also developing local solutions to try to stop people from becoming climate refugees in the first place. These include building flood defences and early warning systems.

▼ Figure 6.20 Which regions are likely to have the most climate refugees?

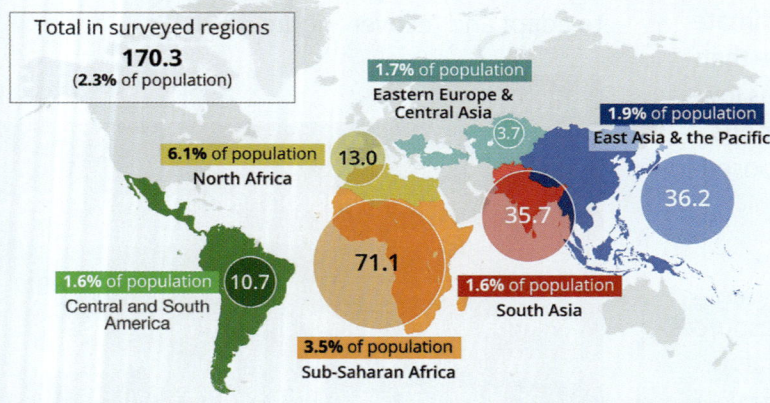

## Climate refugees of the Sundarban Delta

The Sundarban Delta, stretching across India and Bangladesh, is one of the world's most climate-vulnerable regions. Its low-lying islands are threatened by sea-level rise, frequent tropical storms and river erosion, all made worse by climate change. This has led to the displacement of thousands of people, creating a growing population of climate refugees.

About 34 per cent of the population of the Sundarban region live below the **poverty line**, with nearly half unable to afford two full meals a day. The loss of land and livelihoods due to environmental changes leaves

## 6 What impacts will a changing climate have?

these communities with little capacity to adapt or recover, which increases their vulnerability.

Several islands have already disappeared beneath the sea. Thousands have been displaced as erosion and flooding claim more land each year. The government and NGOs have provided some support, such as solar panels and tubewells, but they do not want to invest too much money in case this is also lost.

Figure 6.22 Some tubewells have been provided so that climate refugees can access clean water.

Figure 6.21 A map of the Sundarban region of Bangladesh and India.

### Key terms

**Non-governmental organisations (NGOs):** Non-profit organisations, independent of governments, who work to address social, humanitarian, environmental or development issues globally or locally.

**Poverty line:** The minimum income level needed to afford basic necessities, such as food, shelter and clothing.

**Refugee Convention:** A 1951 UN treaty defining refugees, which outlines their rights and states legal obligations to protect them from persecution.

### Activities

1 Look at Figure 6.20. Which areas of the world are most likely to have people displaced by climate change?

2 Why is it a problem that there is not a proper definition of a 'climate refugee'?

3 Look at Figure 6.21 and find the Sundarban delta in an atlas. Why do you think the people living here might be at risk of the impacts of climate change?

4 Climate refugees are an example where environmental, economic and social impacts interconnect and overlap. Identify as many impacts as you can and then colour code them to suggest whether they are environmental, economic or social (or a mixture).

## 6.8 How will climate change impact Russia?

In this lesson, you are going to explore how climate change impacts a particular country. We have chosen Russia because it is the largest country on Earth and is home to over 140 million people.

### Why is climate change a problem in Russia?

Russia is the largest country in the world and, therefore, it has a large number of diverse environments, ranging from polar ice and tundra in the north, to extensive steppes (grasslands) and arid or dry zones. This diversity means that the impacts of climate change are uneven for the 146 million people who live there. As you saw in the previous lesson, this is likely to increase inequality.

### The thawing of permafrost

About 20 per cent of Russia is within the Arctic Circle, which is warming at more than twice the global average rate. Also, about two thirds of the country is underlain by permafrost. As you discovered in Chapter 1, as permafrost thaws, it destabilises the ground, causing severe damage to buildings, roads, pipelines and entire cities, especially in Siberia. The cost of this damage is severe – estimates suggest $70–100 billion. Thawing permafrost can also destabilise places where radioactive waste has been buried and can also destabilise nuclear power stations, which increases the risk of hazardous material being released. The Norilsk oil spill in 2020 contaminated 350 km$^2$ and was linked to the thawing of permafrost.

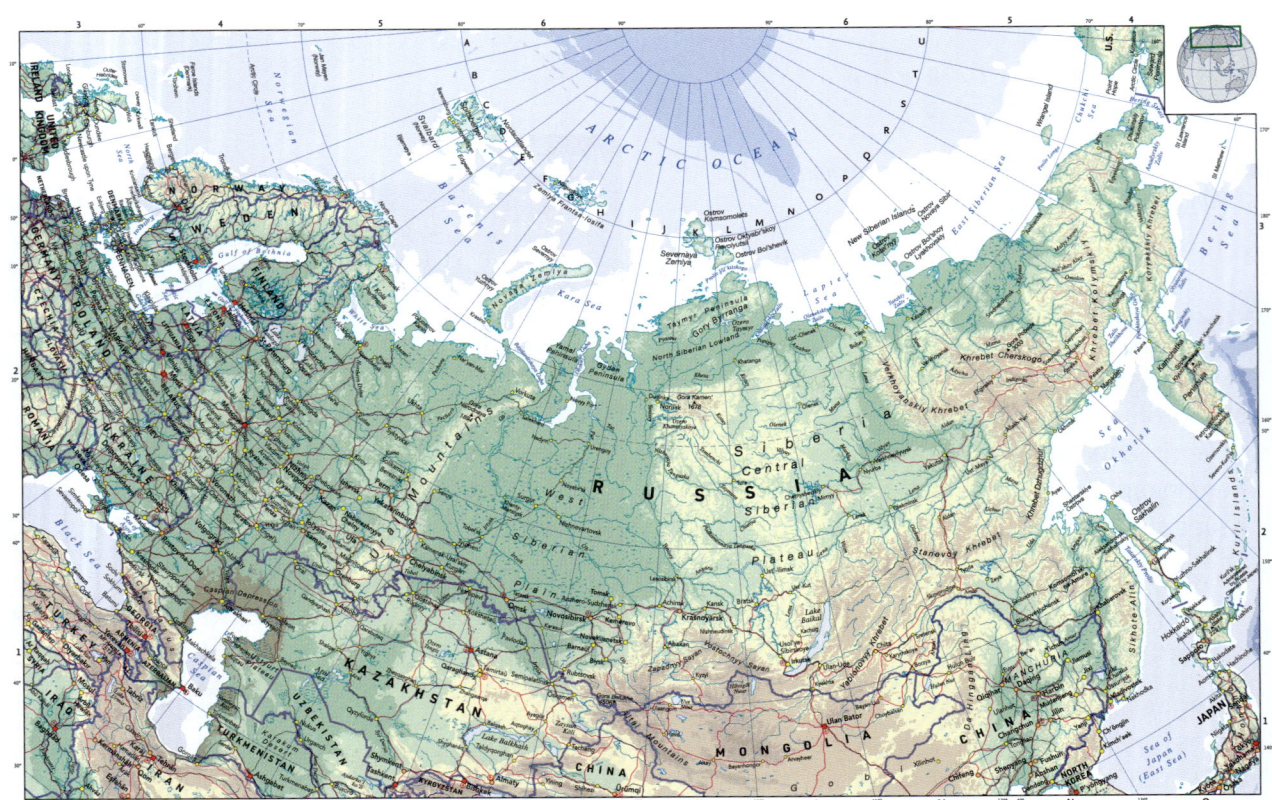

▲ Figure 6.23 Russia's size, location and physical geography make it vulnerable to the impacts of climate change.

## 6 What impacts will a changing climate have?

▲ Figure 6.24 An oil refinery in the Siberian tundra.

## Extreme weather events

Russia's vast landmass exposes it to a wide range of extreme weather events. There are increased wildfires, particularly in Siberia, which have destroyed forests and settlements. There are also more frequent and severe floods, particularly in areas with higher winter precipitation and rapid spring snowmelt. In 2021, Siberia experienced its worst flooding on record, causing $80 million of damage and impacting 23 villages.

However, it is not just the north of the country which is affected. The southern region, where most of Russia's population and farmland are located, is experiencing more droughts and heatwaves. This is threatening food security as wheat yields have become **volatile**.

## Opening Arctic sea routes

Russia is hoping that climate change will bring some positive economic impacts. Shrinking Arctic sea ice is making some of the shipping routes in the region more accessible. It is thought that by 2035, parts of the Arctic will be completely free of ice in the summer.

### Key term

**Volatile**: Situations that are unstable, unpredictable and likely to change suddenly.

The Northern Sea Route (NSR) reduces the shipping distance between Europe and Asia by up to 40 per cent compared with the Suez Canal. There are no travel fees (unlike the Suez Canal), and the route is less congested, offering faster and cheaper shipping.

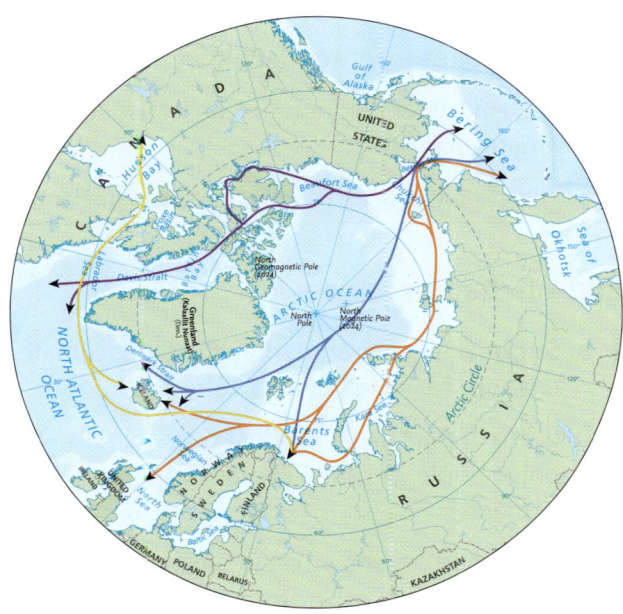

▲ Figure 6.25 Melting Arctic ice is making shipping routes more accessible.

### Activities

1. Look at Figure 6.23. On a blank map of Russia, annotate some of the impacts of climate change.
2. Colour code these annotations to show whether the impacts are environmental, economic or social.
3. 'The impacts of climate change in Russia are negative.' To what extent do you agree with this statement?

# 6 End-of-chapter tasks

## Reflection

1 Why is the idea of planetary health an important one?
2 Who is likely to be most affected by climate change?

## Revision tasks

1 Write a glossary of key definitions from this chapter.
2 Create a spider diagram to summarise some of the environmental, economic and social impacts of climate change.
3 Create a table which summarises the impacts of climate change on Russia.

## End-of-chapter review A

1 a **Suggest** an environmental impact of climate change shown in Figure 6.26. (1 mark)
  b Is this impact likely to affect only animals, only people, or both? **Explain** your answer. (2 marks)
2 a **Name** one city shown on the map (Figure 6.27) that is at a high risk from sea-level rise. (1 mark)

Figure 6.26 A polar bear in the Arctic Circle.

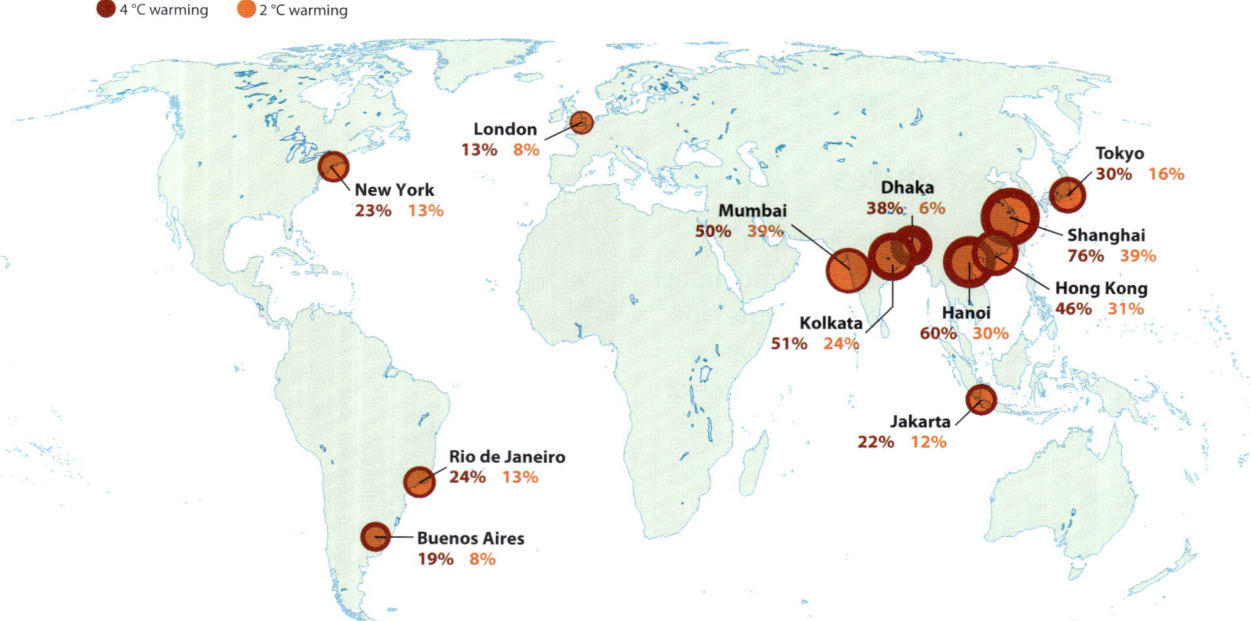

Figure 6.27 The world cities that are most at risk from sea-level rise.

Percentage of population affected by rising sea levels in selected cities in 2010
- 4 °C warming
- 2 °C warming

London 13% 8%
New York 23% 13%
Mumbai 50% 39%
Dhaka 38% 6%
Tokyo 30% 16%
Shanghai 76% 39%
Hong Kong 46% 31%
Kolkata 51% 24%
Hanoi 60% 30%
Jakarta 22% 12%
Rio de Janeiro 24% 13%
Buenos Aires 19% 8%

**b Suggest** one reason why coastal cities are especially vulnerable to climate change. (1 mark)

3 **a Describe** what the graph in Figure 6.28 shows. (3 marks)

**b State** one possible impact of more days above 40 °C for people living in these countries. (1 mark)

4 **a Describe** the type of extreme weather event that is shown in the photograph in Figure 6.29. (2 marks)

**b Explain** two ways this event could impact people and two ways it could impact the environment (4 marks).

5 **To what extent** are the impacts of climate change environmental? (8 marks)

### End-of-chapter review B

How will climate change impact where you live? How is it impacting it already? Use your understanding from the chapter and your own research to find out what the likely impacts of climate change will be in your country. Create a poster which classifies these impacts into positive and negative and into environmental, economic and social. You may also want to weight these impacts or classify them further into short-term or long-term.

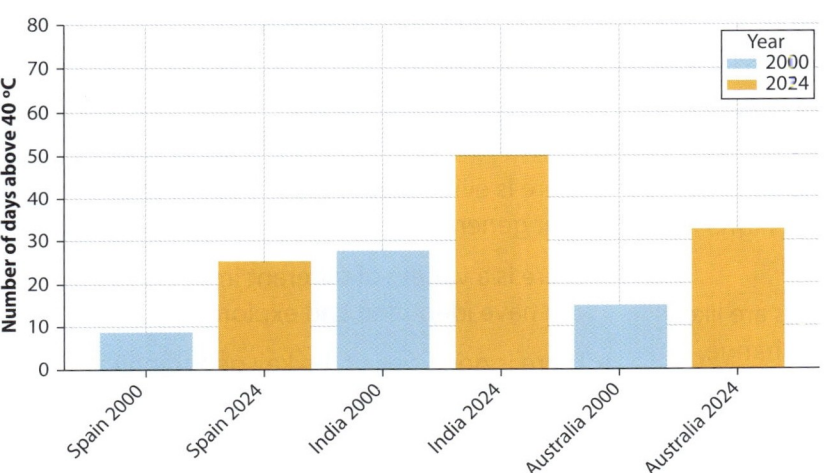

▲ Figure 6.28 The number of days in 2000 and 2024 that were above 40 °C in Spain, India and Australia.

◀ Figure 6.29 Part of the Danube River in Croatia.

# End-of-chapter review support

## End-of-chapter review A

Look at the number of marks available. Where the question is to 'describe', give as many points as there are marks available. Where the question asks you to 'explain', give two points and explain each one. The final question will be marked according to the overall quality of your response.

**1 a** The impact you suggest should have an environmental focus, rather than an economic or social one.

  **b** Decide whether this is an impact on animals, people or both and explain why you think this.

**2 a** Give the name of one of the coastal cities shown on the map that has high percentages of risk from flooding.

  **b** Give one reason why coastal cities are likely to be most impacted by climate change.

**3** The description of the graph has 3 marks, so describe the general trend or pattern and give some specific figures to back up your points.

**4 a** State the type of extreme weather event and what evidence there is from the photo.

  **b** Make two points about people or social impacts and two points about environmental impacts.

**4** A good answer here will:
- make it clear that there are different ways geographers classify impacts
- explain that some of these impacts are environmental, but others are economic or social, or a mixture
- include specific examples of different people/regions that might be particularly affected by climate change
- write a conclusion.

## End-of-chapter review B

A good response to this assessment will have the following features:

- There is evidence of some research to add to your general understanding from this chapter.
- There is a variety of different impacts which you have identified and explored.
- There is good use of the key geographical terms from this chapter.

# Glossary of key terms

**Adapt** – Change to meet a situation.

**Adaptation** – A change made to meet a situation.

**Agriculture** – The practice of cultivating soil, growing crops and raising animals for food, fibre and other products.

**Air pressure** – Force from the weight of the air above a place on the Earth's surface.

**Albedo** – A measure of how much of the Sun's energy a surface reflects.

**Altitude** – Height above sea level. Mountains have a high altitude.

**Aquifer** – Water stored in porous rock below the ground.

**Arid** – Dry, receiving only a small amount of precipitation.

**Artistic inspiration** – The influence of natural landscapes on creative expressions, including visual arts and literature.

**Axis** – An imaginary straight line that an object spins around. The Earth's axis runs through the North and South Poles.

**Biodiversity** – The variety of different plants, animals and other living things in an area, which helps keep ecosystems healthy.

**Biome** – Areas of the planet with similar climate and vegetation.

**Boreal forests** – Conifer forests found in cold climates.

**Citizen science** – Projects that allow regular people to help scientists collect data and conduct research, contributing to scientific knowledge.

**Climate** – The long-term average of weather conditions in a specific place – 'what you expect'.

**Community practices** – Traditions and customs that come from the unique culture of a region, often reflecting local livelihoods.

**Condensation** – Water vapour in the air cools and changes from a gas into liquid water, forming droplets.

**Conservation** – Taking care of nature and protecting plants, animals and their habitats to keep them safe and healthy.

**Crop yields** – How much is produced from an area of land.

**Cultivated** – Grown (plants), usually for commercial purposes.

**Dense** – Crowded.

**Desertification** – The process by which fertile land becomes desert, typically as a result of drought, deforestation or inappropriate agriculture.

**Drainage basin** – An area of land where all surface water flows to a single point, such as a river, lake or ocean.

**Drought** – A period of unusually dry weather that lasts long enough to cause problems such as crop damage and/or water supply shortages.

**Ecosystem** – A community of living organisms interacting with each other and their physical environment.

**Electromagnetic radiation** – Energy that travels through space.

**Emissions** – Substances, usually gases, released into the atmosphere from human activities.

**Encroach** – To slowly move into or take over an area that is usually natural.

**Enhanced greenhouse effect** – Increased warming of the Earth's atmosphere caused by higher concentrations of greenhouse gases due to human activities.

**Entomophagy** – Eating insects as part of the diet.

**Environmental awareness** – Recognising the importance of protecting natural resources and ecosystems

**Erosion** – The wearing away of land by water, wind or ice

**Evaporation** – When liquid water turns into water vapour (gas).

**Exploit** – Remove and use natural resources.

**Export** – Selling food to other countries.

**Extinct** – A species that no longer exists.

**Feedback loop** – A process where a change triggers additional effects that reinforce or counteract the original change.

**Flood risk** – The chance or possibility of an area being covered with water that is not usually there.

**Food bank** – A place where those who are struggling to obtain enough food can go for support and food parcels.

**Food insecurity** – When people do not have regular access enough good food.

**Food miles** – The distance a food item is transported during the journey from producer to consumer.

**Food security** – When people have regular access to enough good food.

**Fresh water** – Found in rivers, lakes, ice sheets and precipitation; it is suitable for drinking.

**GDP** – Stands for Gross Domestic Product, which is the total monetary value of all goods and services produced within a country, usually in a year.

**Geographic Information Systems (GIS)** – Think of GIS as a powerful computer tool that helps to create and analyse maps. It has many 'layers' of information, allowing us to see different aspects of the land, like water flow and land use.

**Glacier** – A large, slow-moving mass of ice.

**Global average temperature** – The average of Earth's surface temperatures, combining measurements from land and oceans.

**Global food supply system (GFSS)** – A complex web of activities involving the production, processing, transport and consumption of food within and between countries.

**Greenhouse gas** – A gas in the Earth's atmosphere that absorbs and traps heat.

**Habitat** – The natural environment where a plant or animal lives.

**Hydroelectric power** – Electricity generated by harnessing the energy of flowing water, often through dams or turbines.

**Hydroelectric power** – Power generated from the movement of water.

**Hydrograph** – A graph showing the discharge of a river over time.

**Impact** – The effect or influence something has on a person or place.

**Import** – Bringing food into a country.

**Inaccessible** – Difficult or impossible to reach and/or use.

**Indigenous people** – Distinct groups descended from the original inhabitants of a place. They maintain unique languages, traditions and strong ties to ancestral lands.

**Industrial Revolution** – A period of major economic and technological change that happened between 1750 and 1900, beginning in Great Britain.

**Inequalities** – Differences in access to resources, opportunities or rights among individuals or groups, often leading to social or economic disadvantage.

**Insulation** – A covering that prevents heat loss.

**Interdependent** – When countries depend on each other.

**Irrigate** – Providing water for farming.

**Irrigation** – The provision of extra water to supplement rainfall to enable crops to be grown.

**Lag time** – The time between peak rainfall and peak river discharge.

**Landscapes** – The visible features of an area of land, including mountains, valleys, rivers and lakes.

**Life expectancy** – The average number of years a person born in a particular place will live.

**Meteorologist** – A scientist who studies the Earth's atmosphere to understand, observe and predict the weather and climate.

**Migrate** – To move from one place to another.

**Milankovitch cycles** – Long-term, natural variations in Earth's orbit that affect how much solar energy the planet receives.

**Mitigate** – Reduce the impact of something.

**Monsoon** – A season with heavy rainfall, common in some parts of the world.

**Nomadic** – People who move from place to place.

**Non-governmental organisations (NGOs)** – Nonprofit organisations, independent of governments, who work to address social, humanitarian, environmental or development issues globally or locally.

**Obesity** – Abnormal or excessive fat accumulation that causes a risk to a person's health.

**Ocean acidification** – The reduction in the pH of the ocean, caused by the absorption of carbon dioxide from the atmosphere due to human activities.

**Outdoor recreation** – Activities that take place in natural environments promoting physical health and community engagement.

**Overgrazing** – When too many animals eat grass and plants in one area, which can damage the soil and reduce plant growth.

**Ozone layer depletion** – The gradual thinning of the ozone layer in the Earth's upper atmosphere caused by human-made chemicals called CFCs.

**Parts per million (ppm)** – A unit of measurement that describes concentrations of $CO_2$ in the atmosphere.

**Peak discharge** – The maximum discharge recorded on a hydrograph.

**Percolate** – Move down through faults or gaps in rock.

**Permafrost** – Permanently frozen soil.

**Photosynthesis** – The process where green plants convert sunlight, carbon dioxide and water into glucose and oxygen, providing energy essential for life.

**Plate tectonics** – The theory that the Earth's outer shell is divided into several plates that glide over the semi-fluid layer beneath.

**Pollution** – The contamination of the environment.

**Population density** – The number of people living in a given area.

**Population** – The total number of people living in an area.

**Poverty line** – The minimum income level needed to afford basic necessities, such as food, shelter and clothing.

**Precipitation** – Water falling to the ground as rain, hail, sleet or snow.

**Pre-industrial average** – The average global temperature between 1850 and 1900, used as the baseline for measuring climate change.

**Prevailing wind** – A wind that blows mostly from the same direction.

**Rate** – In this case, the speed of change.

**Reforestation** – The process of planting trees in an area where forests have been cut down or damaged.

**Refugee Convention** – A 1951 UN treaty defining refugees, which outlines their rights and states legal obligations to protect them from persecution.

**Relief** – The shape of the land. For example, hills and mountains.

**Resilience** – The ability of a system to recover from shocks or setbacks.

**Resource** – Anything that people see as useful or valuable.

**Responsible tourism** – Traveling in a way that respects nature and local cultures, ensuring that our activities do not harm the environment.

**River discharge** – The volume of water flowing through a river channel at any given point.

**Salination** – The process of salt building up in soil or water.

**Satellite** – An object that orbits around a larger body in space.

**Sediment** – Solid material made of grains or fragments of rock that build up in layers.

**Self-sufficient** – When a country can produce all the food it needs, without relying on other countries.

**Soil degradation** – A decline in soil quality, reducing its ability to support plants.

**Soil erosion** – The wearing away of the upper layer of soil, usually by water or wind.

**Soil** – The upper layer of earth in which plants grow.

**Sovereignty** – Power or authority over an area.

**Sparse** – Spread out.

**Standing water** – Stagnant water that collects and provides breeding grounds for mosquitoes.

**Storm surge** – A rise in sea level caused by a storm.

**Sustainability** – Living today in a way which does not affect future generations.

**Sustainability** – The ability to maintain ecological balance by protecting natural resources and the environment, ensuring they can be used by future generations.

**Sustainable tourism** – Travelling in a way that is good for the environment and helps local people, so that beautiful places can be enjoyed by future generations.

**Tap roots** – Long roots of plants that have evolved to reach water deep under the ground.

**Temperate climate** – A climate with moderate temperatures, not too hot or too cold.

**Temperature** – The warmth or coldness of the atmosphere, usually measured in degrees Celsius (°C).

**Terraced farming** – A method of growing crops on the side of a hill or mountain by creating flat areas (terraces) to prevent soil erosion.

**Threshold** – Marks the boundary between one thing and another.

**Tipping point** – Where a threshold is crossed which can lead to large, rapid and irreversible changes.

**Tributary** – A smaller stream or river that flows into a larger river.

**Tropical storms** – Powerful storms in the tropics with heavy rain, strong winds and flooding.

**Tundra** – A cold region where trees do not grow.

**Ultra-processed foods (UPF)** – Food manufactured on an industrial basis, including chemical additives.

**United Nations** – An international organisation founded in 1945 to promote peace, security and cooperation among 193 member countries.

**Vegan** – Choosing to eat a plant-based diet, with no animal-related products, such as milk or eggs.

**Volatile** – Situations that are unstable, unpredictable and likely to change suddenly.

**Volcanic activity** – Processes related to the movement of molten rock from beneath the Earth's crust to the surface, leading to the formation of volcanoes.

**Vulnerable** – A person or place that is more likely to be badly affected by the impacts of climate change.

**Water scarcity** – A lack of sufficient water resources to meet the demands of water usage in a region.

**Water systems** – Networks of water bodies like rivers, lakes and oceans.

**Watershed** – The boundary between two drainage basins.

**Weather** – The condition of the atmosphere at a specific place and time – 'what you get'.

**Weathering** – The breaking down or dissolving of material such as rock at or near the Earth's surface.

**Weathering** – The process of breaking down rocks into smaller pieces by factors like wind, water, temperature changes and biological activity.

**Weight** – How important something is in terms of its impact – some impacts are considered more significant and are given more 'weight'.

**Windward** – The side of a mountain that faces the prevailing wind.